Best Easy Bike Rides
Orange County

Help Us Keep This Guide Up to Date

Every effort has been made by the author and editors to make this guide as accurate and useful as possible. However, many things can change after a guide is published—trails are rerouted, regulations change, techniques evolve, facilities come under new management, etc.

We appreciate hearing from you concerning your experiences with this guide and how you feel it could be improved and kept up to date. While we may not be able to respond to all comments and suggestions, we'll take them to heart and we'll also make certain to share them with the author. Please send your comments and suggestions to the following address:

FalconGuides
Reader Response/Editorial Department
246 Goose Lane, Suite 200
Guilford, CT 06437

Thanks for your input, and happy cycling!

Best Easy Bike Rides Series

Best Easy Bike Rides
Orange County

Wayne D. Cottrell

FALCONGUIDES

GUILFORD, CONNECTICUT

FALCONGUIDES®

An imprint of The Rowman & Littlefield Publishing Group, Inc.
4501 Forbes Blvd., Ste. 200
Lanham, MD 20706
www.rowman.com

Falcon and FalconGuides are registered trademarks and Make Adventure Your Story is a trademark of The Rowman & Littlefield Publishing Group, Inc.

Distributed by NATIONAL BOOK NETWORK

British Library Cataloguing in Publication Information available

Library of Congress Cataloging-in-Publication Data

Names: Cottrell, Wayne D., author.
Title: Best easy bike rides Orange County / Wayne D. Cottrell.
Description: Lanham, MD : FalconGuides, [2020] | Includes bibliographical references and index.
Identifiers: LCCN 2020029558 (print) | LCCN 2020029559 (ebook) | ISBN 9781493052417 (paperback) | ISBN 9781493052424 (epub)
Subjects: LCSH: Bicycle touring–California–Orange County–Guidebooks. | Orange County (Calif.)–Guidebooks.
Classification: LCC GV1045.5.C22 O734 2020 (print) | LCC GV1045.5.C22 (ebook) | DDC 796.6409794/96–dc23
LC record available at https://lccn.loc.gov/2020029558
LC ebook record available at https://lccn.loc.gov/2020029559

To my son, Tyler; to Jerry; and to the memory of my mother, Barbara, and my grandmother Louella

Contents

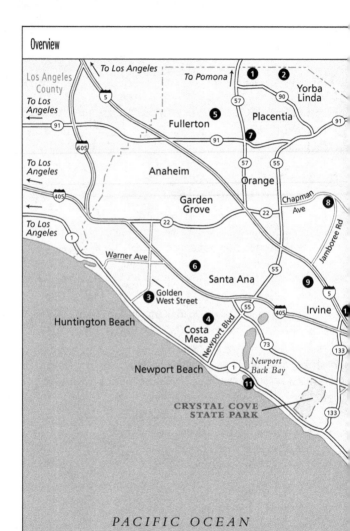

Overview

Los Angeles County

To Los Angeles

To Pomona

To Los Angeles

Yorba Linda

Placentia

Fullerton

Anaheim

Orange

Garden Grove

Chapman Ave

Jamboree Rd

Warner Ave

Santa Ana

Golden West Street

Irvine

Huntington Beach

Costa Mesa

Newport Blvd

Newport Beach

Newport Back Bay

CRYSTAL COVE STATE PARK

PACIFIC OCEAN

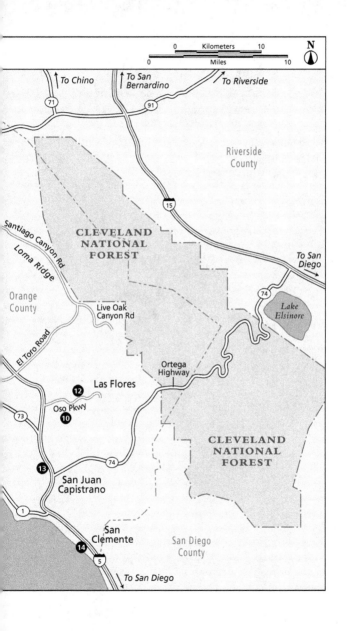

Abstract

This book offers fifteen easy bicycle rides, plus ten suggested (also easy) rides, of various lengths and terrain to cover a wide range of abilities. The rides are generally short in length, in keeping with the book's easy theme. None of the rides has long or steep climbs. It is nearly impossible to encounter entirely flat routes, though—especially in Orange County— so many of the rides feature a few short climbs and descents. The book is designed for entry-level and beginner cyclists, and riders who are not prepared or do not have the time for a long route. Yet, fit cyclists can find some fun and training in doing any of these rides fast, or maybe two or more times in succession. The Orange County region is relatively compact, with an area just under 1,000 square miles. Corey Schlom's *The Unseen OC* suggests, however, that there are sides of Orange County with which few are familiar, even within its relatively small space. This book exposes the popular spots and some lesser-known corners of the county. The twenty-five rides are evenly split between road and mountain routes. The rides highlighted here show why Orange County remains one of the top US biking destinations.

Introduction

Orange County is statistically and geographically part of the expansive Los Angeles–Long Beach–Anaheim Metropolitan Area. Its population of just over three million in 2010 represented 20% of the Los Angeles urbanized area's population, and Orange County was the sixth most populous county in the United States. Orange County is small and compact by Southern California standards, with an area of just 948 square miles. The county's geography is characterized as an extension of the Los Angeles Basin in the north and west, and the Santa Ana Mountains in the east, which rise to 5,687 feet (Santiago Peak). In between the basin and the mountains is Loma Ridge, which runs parallel to the Santa Anas along the eastern edge of the basin, separated from the Santa Anas by Santiago Canyon. The foothills of the Santa Ana Mountains tend to dominate the southern part of the county, with Saddleback Valley being the most prominent low-lying expanse. There is essentially no geographic barrier between L.A. and Orange Counties.

Despite extensive and ongoing development in Orange County, "hidden" areas remain comparatively untouched, including the Santa Ana Mountains, most of Loma Ridge, and various enclaves and nooks. A significant amount of land has been preserved for natural habitats, including an extensive regional park system, open spaces of the Irvine Ranch Conservancy, and Cleveland National Forest. Bicycling in Orange County is popular and thriving, in part because of the year-round Mediterranean weather that is an attraction of the entire Los Angeles region. Packs of cyclists can be seen riding the roads in Irvine, along the Pacific coast, and in Santiago Canyon on a regular basis. There are several long, car-free bicycle paths in the county, and most of the newer roads—particularly those in the southern part of the county—feature bike lanes. Off-road cycling is permitted on nearly all of the trails in the regional parks and in Cleveland National Forest; a limited amount of off-road riding is available in the Irvine Ranch Conservancy's open spaces.

About Orange County

Orange County is heavily urbanized, but there is no major central city. There are thirty-four incorporated cities; Anaheim is the largest at 350,365 persons in 2019. The county seat, Santa Ana, is nearly as populous (332,318 in 2019). Two other cities have populations of 200,000 or more (Huntington Beach and Irvine), and four others have populations of 100,000 or more (Costa Mesa, Fullerton, Garden Grove, and Orange). The county's economy was originally based on cattle ranching, until the late 1880s, when silver was discovered in the Santa Ana Mountains. Soon after settlers started flocking to the area, the county was separated from Los Angeles County (1889). Agriculture also became vital, particularly citrus fruits and avocados, as well as oil extraction. With transportation improvements, which initially featured the railroad and electric trolleys, and later highways, Orange County became attractive as a Los Angeles suburb, as well as a getaway for prosperous Los Angelenos. The economy transformed after World War II with this growth and was given a boost with the opening of Disneyland in 1955.

Today, Orange County's economy is dependent on tourism, technology, medicine, entertainment, and education. Several major US and international companies are headquartered here. A system of toll freeways generates hundreds of millions of dollars in revenue annually. The county declared bankruptcy in 1994 but has been able to recover and thrive, tapping into its many resources. As for tourism, Orange County's top spots include Disneyland, Knott's Berry Farm, and the beaches, plus plenty of other attractions, including Crystal Cathedral, Orange County Zoo, the Richard M. Nixon Birthplace and Museum, and others. There is plenty to see in Orange County by bicycle, via the county's expansive network of trails, bikeways, and roads that are suitable for bikes. The reader is encouraged to do the rides in this book and then try those in *Best Bike Rides Orange County*!

About This Book

The twenty-five rides described include fourteen in northern Orange County and eleven in the south. The terrain is slightly easier in the north than in the south, hence the imbalance. There is a map and Miles and Directions section for fifteen of the rides and a text description for the other ten. Each ride's text includes the route (roads and trails), road and trail conditions, traffic information, and descriptions of scenery, history, folklore, special events, culture, flora, and fauna along the way so that the rider knows what to expect. The descriptions give each route character. To keep the rider in the present, the descriptions also discuss demographics, urban issues, and transport infrastructure. To orient the user, the GPS coordinates of each start-finish point are included. Information on climb lengths and gradients are included as well.

Resources

The key bicycling organizations are the Orange County Transportation Authority (550 South Main Street, Orange; 715–560–OCTA; www.octa.net) and the Orange County Bicycle Coalition (1900 North El Camino Real, San Clemente; 949–492–5737; www.ocbike.org). A number of cities have developed bike plans and/or bikeway networks, including Anaheim, Fullerton, Irvine, Lake Forest, San Juan Capistrano, Santa Ana, and Yorba Linda, while still others have developed off-road trail networks, including Laguna Niguel and San Clemente. Each of these cities may also have bicycling specialists among their planning and engineering personnel. The SoCalCycling website (http://socalcycling.com) has information on racing, clubs, bike shops, products, events, and other resources. The region is home to a host of bicycling clubs, ranging from recreational riders to serious racing teams—an excellent list is provided at http://socalcycling.com/clubs-teams. Bicycle shops are also great resources—a fine list is at http://socalcycling.com/bike-shops; also, each ride in this book is followed by information on one or more nearby bike shops. The Orange County Bicycle Coalition also has lists of clubs and shops on its website. Do not hesitate to treat the region's riders as resources, as many of them are quite knowledgeable.

Safety and Equipment

For most of the road routes contained in this book, traffic ranges from minimal to medium-heavy, depending on the time of day you are riding and the day of the week. To be safe, it is paramount to be predictable. If motorists have a good sense of what to expect from you, you'll be safer on the road. Riding with traffic, signaling turns, and generally obeying the same rules that apply to motor traffic are great habits. For the novice, riding with traffic in Orange County can be easy, especially if there is an adequate shoulder on the road. Riding is even easier when there is a bike lane, and easiest when there is a separated bike path.

The door zone—the area where car doors swing open—should be avoided, even if that requires riding farther into the traffic lane. Similarly, you have the right to take the lane when avoiding potholes or other obstacles on the roadside, and you always have the right of way along a "sharrow" (shared traffic lane). Cyclists are advised to use special caution at intersections, where drivers make left and right turns. One approach is to assume that drivers do not see you, even when a traffic control gives you the right of way.

Busy bicycle paths, such as the Santa Ana River Trail, can have a mixture of users, including pedestrians, slow and fast cyclists, recumbent riders, in-line skaters, step-gliders, and others. Some paths separate cyclists from other users, but do not depend on adherence to this. Be alert to all users and treat paths as shared facilities. If you are a beginning cyclist, then a bike safety class can be useful. People who participate in a good class consistently express how much safer and more comfortable they feel riding in a variety of traffic conditions. Cycling courses also cover other topics, such as bike selection and fit, basics of bike handling, and maintenance.

What should you bring on your ride? Always pack a pump and spare tube or patch kit. A small multi-tool will help with adjustments and minor repairs. Bring lights for front and back—some cyclists use these at all times, including daylight. Bring water, something to snack on, and one more layer than you think you'll need, particularly in cooler weather. With a cell phone and some cash or card, you are ready to go!

How to Use This Guide

When choosing rides in this book, observe the length, the net elevation difference, the total amount of climbing, and the range of ride times. Road rides range from 5.45 to 15.3 miles. Mountain bike rides range from 3.4 to 7.3 miles. All of the rides in the book have a high-low elevation differential of less than 375 feet. Much of Orange County is hilly, though, so these rides are the exception rather than the rule, in terms of their lack of longer climbs. The Ride Finder section lists the distribution of ride distances and elevation changes. The easiest rides, and the best ones to do with children, use bike paths, have less than 100 feet of climbing, and are short in mileage. Note that rides can be improvised by turning around early or by doing two laps of a route rather than one. Divide the elevation differential by the distance: the higher the value, the more challenging the ride.

UTM coordinates: Readers who use either a handheld or car-mounted GPS unit can punch in the UTM coordinates for each starting point and have the GPS lead the way. The UTM coordinates are to be used with NAD 27 datum (rather than WGS 83 or WGS 84).

Mileage markers on the map: The distances provided in the book may not match up with distances provided by existing trail maps or your own bike odometer. If you are using a bike odometer, note that it must be calibrated carefully; changing to a larger tire can make a noticeable difference. Although GPS devices are generally accurate, they too can be off. Use the mileage data in this book as a rough guide that provides you with a close—but not exact—determination of distance traveled.

Traffic volumes: For the roads ridden in this book, a year 2018 (unless otherwise noted) twenty-four-hour, two-way traffic volume is provided. Traffic volumes vary by hour of the day, day of the week, location, and season, so the average is representative of the given road segment. A daily traffic volume of under 5,000 is light; 5,000 to 15,000 is medium; 15,000 to 25,000 is medium-heavy; and 25,000 and over is heavy. Some routes use heavily trafficked roads out of necessity, for the scenery, or for the experience.

Times: To assist cyclists with ride planning, a range of estimated times (fast and leisurely) is provided for each ride. My time for the route is also provided and can be used as a benchmark. Note that my times include all stops at traffic signals and stop signs.

Highway, Street, Path, and Trail Names

Highway and street names are taken from street maps and signs. State highways are abbreviated CA. The Pacific Coast Highway, which is CA 1, is commonly referred to as PCH by locals. Path names are not always evident, but some of those in Orange County are painted onto the path at spaced intervals. There may also be small signs posted at entry points and junctions. Underpasses are often indicated by an overhead sign. Trails in Orange County's regional parks are well marked. Other trails and paths may be marked sporadically or not at all. The mileage logs and text descriptions attempt to convey the proper directions, to keep you on course.

Road Surface, Shoulder, Path, and Trail Conditions

The road and path surfaces in these rides are, in general, in good condition, unless otherwise noted. Shoulders and shoulder widths are adequate unless otherwise noted. Trail conditions can vary according to the season, level of usage, rainfall and drainage, and maintenance. Some of the trails in the regional parks, and those used by equestrians, can have moguls and exposed and/or loose rocks. Erosion can occur over time, creating fissures. Note that park trails are closed for three days following a rainstorm. Trails can also be closed because of brush fires, construction, or maintenance work.

How to Use the Maps

Each ride map illustrates the given route and starting/ending point against a backdrop of important roads, geographical features, communities, and landmarks. The maps include a limited amount of information, by intention, to emphasize the given route. Selected mile markers, along with the recommended direction of travel, are included on each map. For out-and-back segments, the mile markers generally pertain to the outbound direction of travel. The total length of the ride is listed near the starting/ending point. The scales of the maps vary. If you need more detailed map and location information, then please refer to the "Map" entry in each ride's header section.

Map Legend

Transportation

═══⑤═══	Interstate/Divided Highway
━━━①━━━	Featured State Road
─⟨57⟩─	State Highway
───────	County/Local Road
▪▪▪▪▪▪▪▪▪▪	Featured Bike Route
▬▬▬▬▬	Featured Paved Route
···········	Trail/Unpaved Road
⊢─┼─┤	Railroad

Hydrology

⬭	Lake/Reservoir/Major River
⌇	River

Symbols

⊃⊂	Bridge
🎓	College
49'	Elevation
⌶	Gate
1.3 ◆─	Mileage Marker
🅿	Parking
■	Point of Interest/Structure
❶	Trailhead (Start)

Land Use

▭	National Forest
▭	State or Local Park

Ride Finder

Ride	No.	Miles	Bike	Region	Elev. Differential
Angeles del Centro Santa Ana	16	7.9	road	north	99 ft
Arroyo Trabuco Sur-cuit	10	5.75	mtn	south	243 ft
Baker Ranch Promenade	17	5.55	road	south	177 ft
Balboa Peninsula Tour	18	10.15	road	north	7 ft
Brea Tracks to La Habra	1	13.25	road	north	184 ft
Capistrano's Crowl Prowl	19	4.6	mtn	south	248 ft
Carbon Canyon Dust-Up	2	6.0	mtn	north	292 ft
Central Park Discs to Dobbins	3	3.4	mtn	north	58 ft
Coastin' Costa Mesa	20	13.25	road	north	47 ft
Corona to Crystal Shoreline Ride	11	7.1	road	south	79 ft
Costa Mesa Cruise	4	4.25	mtn	north	62 ft
Cycle Serrano Creek	21	6.3	mtn	south	371 ft
Fullerton Pump & Circumstance	5	6.8	road	north	94 ft
Meandering Ladera Ridge	12	4.05	mtn	south	307 ft
Mile Square Squall	6	5.45	road	north	18 ft
Oso Sweet SJC Trails Ride	13	4.8	mtn	south	173 ft

Ride	No.	Miles	Bike	Region	Elev. Differential
Plateau Placentia	7	10.65	road	north	217 ft
San Clemente Beach Boogie	14	5.85	mtn	south	156 ft
San Onofre Bluffs Blast	22	7.3	mtn	south	163 ft
Santa Ana River Diversion	23	8.5	mtn	north	59 ft
Santiago Hills, Oaks & Spokes	8	5.75	mtn	north	150 ft
Seal Beach Wildlife to Weapons Loop	24	15.3	road	north	33 ft
Tour d'El Toro	15	11.6	road	south	280 ft
Upper Irvine–Northwood Nexus	9	14.8	road	north	252 ft
Velo Capistrano	25	9.4	road	south	269 ft

Best Easy Northern Orange County Rides

Orange County's most notable geographic features are the coastline, Santa Ana River, and Santa Ana Mountains. There are no evident subregions, though. One loose form of subregion division is to look at when Orange County's cities incorporated. The older cities tend to be in the northwest, with a few exceptions, while the newer cities tend to be in the southeast. Only two of the cities in the south, Laguna Beach and San Clemente, incorporated before 1929. The rest of the "old" cities—Anaheim (1870—the oldest), Brea (1917), Fullerton (1904), Huntington Beach (1909), La Habra (1925), Newport Beach (1906), Orange (1888), Placentia (1926), Santa Ana (1886), Seal Beach (1915), and Tustin (1927)—are in the northwest, or north. Although, Newport Beach and Irvine, the county's two largest cities by area, straddle the imaginary northern-southern Orange County boundary. Adding in cities that were incorporated between 1953 and 1967 (Buena Park, Costa Mesa, Cypress, Fountain Valley, Garden Grove, La Palma, Los Alamitos, Stanton, Villa Park, Westminster, and Yorba Linda, along with several unincorporated communities) produces an area of 315 square miles, and a 2019 population of 2,173,200. So, 70% of Orange County's population lives in 40% of its area.

Although northern Orange County is heavily urbanized, there are a few nice open spaces, such as the Bolsa Chica

Ecological Reserve in Huntington Beach, the Seal Beach Wildlife Refuge, and Santiago Oaks and Irvine Regional Parks in Orange. Orange (city) is the gateway to Santiago Canyon, with Loma Ridge (mostly protected and inaccessible) at the foothills of the Santa Ana Mountains (mostly but not entirely accessible). Paved bike paths serve the area, including ones along Coyote Creek, near the Los Angeles County border, and Santiago Creek, which is central. There is also the well-known Santa Ana River Trail, which extends across the entire county. The city of Fullerton has a network of dirt trails that connect parks and small open spaces. Premium attractions such as Disneyland have limited bicycle accessibility. But, elsewhere, northern Orange County has plenty of easy bike riding, in terms of the five road and four mountain routes described below.

1   Brea Tracks to La Habra

Start: Country Hills Park, 180 North Associated Road, Brea
Length: 13.25 miles (lollipop-shaped route—long loop and short stick)
Riding time: 45 to 120 minutes (my time: 57:07)
Terrain and surface: 67% paved roads, 31% paved paths, and 2% concrete walkways (plus one downward staircase)
Elevations: Low—229 feet at Lambert Road and Villageglen Lane in La Habra; high—413 feet at Central Avenue and Berry Street in Brea
Traffic and hazards: Daily traffic volumes in La Habra were 37,000 on Lambert Road near Palm Street and 3,000 on Idaho Street north of Lambert Road. In Brea they were 34,000 on La Habra Boulevard west of Brea Boulevard and 15,000 on Brea Boulevard at the Trail at Brea Tracks.

Map: *The Thomas Guide by Rand McNally—Street Guide: Los Angeles and Orange Counties* (any recent year), page 709
Getting there by car: From central Anaheim, head north on CA 57 freeway. Exit at Lambert Road and turn right. Turn right on Associated Road and head south. Look for Country Hills Park on the left, opposite Sleepy Hollow Lane.
Getting there by public transit: Orange County Transportation Authority (OCTA) bus route 129 travels between Anaheim and La Habra along Kraemer Boulevard and Birch Street. Exit bus at Birch Street and Associated Road. Head north on Associated; Country Hills Park will be on the right. Route 129 runs every 55 to 70 minutes daily.
Starting point coordinates: 33.920472°N / 117.871986°W

The Ride

Brea Tracks to La Habra is a 13.25-mile road ride, through the cities of Brea and La Habra. The total amount of climbing is 313 feet. A ride feature is the Tracks at Brea Trail, which is a new, as of this writing, rail-to-trail conversion. Such reuses of old railroad infrastructure started in the 1960s, when folks simply started walking along railroad rights-of-way. The paved trail is just over 2 miles, with plans to lengthen it in the future. The route design is a 1.8-mile out-and-back segment, of which 1.45 miles is on the Tracks at Brea Trail, plus a 9.65-mile clockwise loop, of which 0.25 miles is on the trail. Most of the loop (5.45 miles) is in La Habra, which had an estimated population of 62,180 in 2018. The city is located in the far northwest corner of Orange County and is bordered on the west and north by Los Angeles County. Given that, the city shares characteristics with L.A. County cities, including a population that is more than 55% Hispanic and emergency services provided by L.A. rather than Orange County. The ride passes La Habra High School along Highlander Avenue. Notable graduates of LHHS include Paul

THE BREA TRACKS

The Brea Trail—more formally, the Tracks at Brea Trail—is a new (as of this writing), 50-acre linear park that will extend 4 miles across the city of Brea. In a true rails-to-trails conversion, the city has redeveloped an old rail line, turning it into a two-lane bike and foot path! The railroad was built by the Pacific Electric Railway in 1910 as the Yorba Linda Branch. The line served the oil fields and citrus groves that were abundant in the area at the time. Later, many of those oil fields shut down, and the groves were replaced by residential and commercial development. That led to the downsizing of the line, and the cutbacks—by a mile or two at a time—continued into the early twenty-first century. The last stretch of track was removed in 2009, enabling the transformation of the right-of-way. There are plans to extend the current trail beyond its dead-end bulb-out.

McCartney guitarist Rusty Anderson, 1994 Miss California Jennifer Hanson, Air National Guard Brigadier General John N. Lotz, and 2004 Olympic softball gold medalist Jenny Topping. Brea had an estimated population of 43,600 in 2018, up 11% since 2010. At the close of this ride's loop, the route turns left off of Brea Boulevard onto the Tracks at Brea Trail for the return trip. Just ahead on Brea, though, is the city's vibrant central district. A visit there, particularly for evening activities, is highly recommended.

Miles and Directions

0.0 Start in Country Hills Park in Brea—exit the park; turn left onto Associated Road.

0.2 Traffic signal at Birch Street—turn right; ride onto the walkway.

0.35 Right onto the Trail at Brea Tracks (paved path).

0.8 Pass under CA 57 freeway.

0.95 At-grade crossings of State College Boulevard and Brea Boulevard (mile 1.8).

2.05 Veer left off bike path; hoist bike, walk down the stairs.

2.1 Remount; continue riding (paved path).

2.25 Right onto bridge—keep straight onto Mercury Street.

2.45 Stop sign at Berry Street—turn right.

2.55 Railroad crossing (one track).

2.75 Traffic signal at Lambert Road—turn left.

3.00 Traffic signal at Delta Avenue and at Puente Street (mile 3.25)—keep straight.

3.45 Enter the city of La Habra.

3.55 Lambert Road narrows from six to four lanes.

3.75 Traffic signal at Palm Street, at a retail center (mile 4.15), and at Harbor Boulevard (mile 4.25)—keep straight on Lambert at each intersection.

3.85 Railroad crossings, also at miles 4.05 and 4.55—track is skewed at the first crossing.

5.05 Traffic signal at Euclid Street—begin bike lane; keep straight.

5.3 Traffic signal at Walnut Street—keep straight.

5.7 Cross Villageglen Lane—lowest elevation of ride (229 feet).

5.8 Traffic signal at Idaho Street; turn right—all roads from here to Palm Street are Class III bike routes.

6.05 Railroad crossing.

6.3 Cross La Habra Boulevard—Idaho Street narrows from four to two lanes.

6.55 Right on Highlander Avenue.

7.05 Stop sign at Walnut Street—turn left.

7.1 Right on Greenwood Avenue.

7.2 Right on Rose Avenue; Rose curves left to head east.

7.5 Stop sign at Orange Street—turn right.

7.6 Left on Florence Avenue.

7.85 Stop sign at Lemon Street—turn right.

7.95 Left on Erna Avenue.

8.05 Stop sign at McPherson Street—turn left.

8.1 Right on Stearns Avenue.

8.8 Stop sign at Palm Street—turn right.

8.9 Traffic signal at La Habra Boulevard; turn left—end of Class III bike routes (La Habra has bike lane).

9.15 Re-enter Brea; now on Central Avenue.

9.9 Cross Berry Street—highest elevation of ride (413 feet).

10.65 Traffic signal at Brea Boulevard—turn right.

11.15 Traffic signal at Lambert Road—keep straight.

Brea Tracks to La Habra

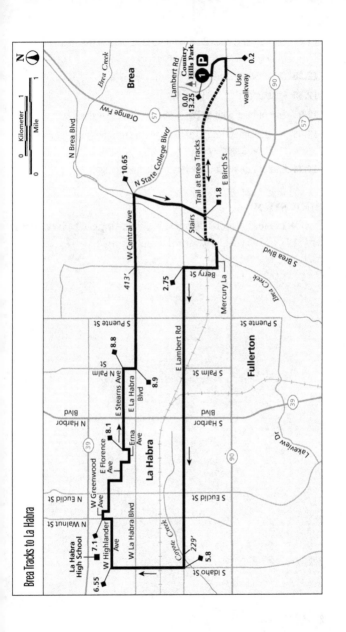

N

Brea

Brea Creek

Country Hills Park

Lambert Rd

1 P

0.0/ 13.25

Use walkway

0.2

Orange Fwy

57

N Brea Blvd

90

57

N State College Blvd

10.65

Trail at Brea Tracks

1.8

E Birch St

W Central Ave

Stairs

S Brea Blvd

Brea Creek

413'

2.75

Berry St

Mercury La

S Puente St

S Puente St

E Lambert Rd

Fullerton

8.8

8.9

E Stearns Ave

N Palm St

E La Habra Blvd

S Palm St

N Harbor Blvd

8.1

Erna Ave

E Florence Ave

W Greenwood Ave

S Harbor Blvd

39

W Walnut St

N Euclid St

S Euclid St

La Habra

90

Lakeview Dr

La Habra High School

7.1

W Highlander Ave

W La Habra Blvd

Coyote Creek

229'

6.55

5.8

S Idaho St

0   Kilometer   1

0   Mile   1

11.4 Left to cross over Brea Boulevard to access the Trail at Brea Tracks—now on return route.

12.25 Cross State College Boulevard.

12.45 Pass under CA 57 freeway.

12.9 End of bike path at Birch Street; left onto walkway.

13.05 At Associated Road (traffic signal), cross and turn left; head north on Associated.

13.25 End of ride at Country Hills Park, on the right.

BIKE SHOP

Two Wheeler Dealer Bicycles, 1039 E. Imperial Hwy., Brea, (714) 671–1730, www.twdcycling.com

2 Carbon Canyon Dust-Up

Start: Olinda Ranch Park, Carbon Canyon Road (CA 142) at Santa Fe, Brea
Length: 6.0 miles (two clockwise loops, connected by a middle "neck")
Riding time: 30 to 75 minutes (my time: 61:38 on foot)
Terrain and surface: 83% dirt trails, 11% paved roads, and 6% paved paths
Elevations: Low—410 feet on unnamed trail in Carbon Canyon Regional Park; high—702 feet on Redwood Grove Trail
Traffic and hazards: CA 142 was carrying 18,000 vehicles daily at Carbon Canyon Regional Park.
Map: *The Thomas Guide by Rand McNally—Street Guide: Los Angeles and Orange Counties* (any recent year), page 709
Getting there by car: From central Anaheim, head north on CA 57 freeway. Exit at Lambert Road and turn right. Lambert Road becomes Carbon Canyon Road after crossing Valencia Avenue. Turn left on Santa Fe Road, opposite Carbon Canyon Regional Park. Climb hill; turn left on Railway Avenue. At fork, bear left onto Weeping Willow Road. Enter park to the right.
Getting there by public transit: No transit service available
Starting point coordinates: 33.920028°N / 117.825606°W

The Ride

Carbon Canyon Dust-Up is a 6.0-mile mountain bike ride on trails in Carbon Canyon Regional Park in Brea and the adjacent Vista del Verde community in Yorba Linda. The total amount of climbing is 470 feet, which is on the high end for an easy ride. The title refers to carbon dust, which was present in this vicinity during the heavier oil-drilling days of yore. Drilling continues today but has been reduced as local reserves are tapped. Start from Olinda Ranch Park, which

REDWOOD TREES IN CARBON CANYON?

Wait—redwood trees in Orange County, in Southern California? Sequoia sempervirens are indigenous to coastal California and the southern corner of Oregon, occupying a strip that is about 500 miles long and up to 40 miles wide. The domain of the trees extends as far south as Monterey, California. Brea is 20 miles from the ocean, which is within the coastal bandwidth, but is over 350 miles south of Monterey! So, how did a grove of redwoods sprout up in Carbon Canyon Regional Park? Some sources say that the grove covers 3 acres, while others say 10; in either case, the trees do not flourish without attention. Redwoods do not grow naturally in Southern California because of the lack of rainfall. The grove was planted in 1975 and needs plenty of artificial irrigation to survive. In tree years, they are still quite young. The typical tree height in the grove is only about 100 feet. This compares to the 300-foot (or more) behemoths found in natural redwood locations. Yet, even these mini-redwoods are marvelous to view. There are about 200 trees in the grove, although one of them had been "put down," as of this writing, because of the effects of an ongoing drought.

is on the diagonally opposite side of Carbon Canyon Road from the regional park. Immediately head toward Carbon Canyon Regional Park, to begin a loop around the park's perimeter. The south side of the park is bordered by a steep hillside. High above is the Vista del Verde community, where the ride is headed; several residences there overlook the park. The route then passes Redwood Grove (please see sidebar). The park loop is interrupted by a loop of Vista del Verde. Getting there requires climbing a 300-foot, 15.5% grade hill. You will enter the city of Yorba Linda halfway up the hill. Yorba Linda had an estimated population of 67,780 in 2018, up 6% from 2010. The city is most famous as the childhood home of former US president Richard Nixon. Once back in the park, the route passes Carbon Canyon Dam, which is massive, despite the lack of water. The dam is there should Carbon Canyon Creek ever reach flood stage.

Miles and Directions

0.0 Start the ride in the lower section of Olinda Ranch Park—exit the park via the path; head east, adjacent to Carbon Canyon Road.

0.2 Cross Santa Fe Road, and then Carbon Canyon Road (traffic signal), to enter Carbon Canyon Regional Park via the trail.

0.25 Trail dissipates into open grass area—continue straight to park road.

0.3 Head eastward on paved park road.

0.6 Stay right upon entering parking lot.

0.7 Keep straight onto Carbon Canyon Creek Nature Trail.

0.75 Trail curves right.

0.85 Trail dips to cross (usually dry) Carbon Canyon Creek, and then curves right to head west.

1.6 Trail bends 90° left.

1.75 Redwood Grove at right.

1.9 Trail curves right (Redwood Grove perimeter).

1.95 Left onto connector trail—315-foot climb (15.5% grade).

2.0 Top of climb; left onto Redwood Grove Trail.

2.2 Bear left; continue on Redwood Grove Trail—begin clockwise upper loop.

2.25 After short descent, trail climbs gradually at 3.2% grade.

2.55 Keep straight at merge; trail then makes a couple of curves to the right.

3.15 Crest of trail—highest elevation of the ride (702 feet); begin descent.

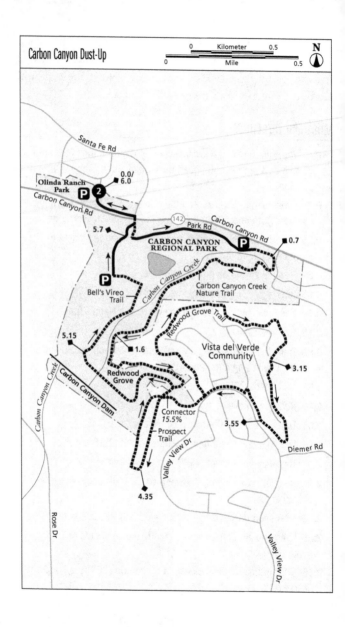

Carbon Canyon Dust-Up

0   Kilometer   0.5
0   Mile   0.5

N

Santa Fe Rd

Olinda Ranch Park

0.0/6.0

Carbon Canyon Rd

142 Park Rd Carbon Canyon Rd

5.7

CARBON CANYON REGIONAL PARK

0.7

Bell's Vireo Trail

Carbon Canyon Creek

Carbon Canyon Creek Nature Trail

5.15

Redwood Grove Trail

1.6

Vista del Verde Community

3.15

Carbon Canyon Creek

Carbon Canyon Dam

Redwood Grove

Connector 15.5%

3.55

Prospect Trail

Diemer Rd

4.35

Valley View Dr

Rose Dr

Valley View Dr

3.45 Cross paved access road.

3.55 Stay right, and then bear left at forks.

3.75 Trail break at Red Pine Road; cross road, turn left and then right to resume trail.

4.1 Keep straight at trail junction—now on Prospect Trail.

4.35 Right at unnamed trail—short climb.

4.4 Right onto unnamed trail—now on upper mesa, parallel to Prospector Trail (below you).

4.6 Return to trail junction; left onto connector trail—steep descent (15.5% grade).

4.65 Base of descent; left to re-enter Carbon Canyon Regional Park; Redwood Grove at right.

4.9 Trail curves right—lowest elevation of ride (410 feet).

5.1 Continue through open space; Carbon Creek Dam at left.

5.15 Right onto Bell's Vireo Trail.

5.35 Stay left at trail junction.

5.4 End of trail—bear left, enter gravel parking lot.

5.55 Curve right; continue through paved lot and onto park road.

5.7 Short uphill to exit park.

5.75 Cross Carbon Canyon Road (traffic signal), and then turn left to cross Santa Fe Road—keep straight onto paved path.

6.0 Re-enter Olinda Ranch Park to conclude ride.

BIKE SHOP

Two Wheeler Dealer Bicycles, 1039 E. Imperial Hwy., Brea, (714) 671–1730, www.twdcycling.com

3   Central Park Discs to Dobbins

Start: Central Park (Dog Park entrance), Inlet Drive east of Edwards Street, Huntington Beach

Length: 3.4 miles (clockwise loop with zigs and zags)

Riding time: 30 to 55 minutes (my time: 44:22 on foot)

Terrain and surface: 76% dirt trails and 24% paved park paths

Elevations: Low—6 feet at Dog Park; high—64 feet in equestrian trails area

Traffic and hazards: 100% of the ride is on car-free park paths and trails. Give way to equestrians on trails.

Map: *The Thomas Guide by Rand McNally—Street Guide: Los Angeles and Orange Counties* (any recent year), page 857

Getting there by car: From central Anaheim, head south on either I-5 or CA 57. Exit to CA 22 freeway. Exit at Knott Avenue/ Golden West Street and turn left (onto Golden West). Right on Ellis Avenue, then right at Edwards Street. Right on Inlet Drive. Enter Central Park at first entrance on right.

Getting there by public transit: OCTA bus route 76 runs between John Wayne Orange County Airport and Huntington Beach, via MacArthur Boulevard and Talbert Avenue. Exit the bus at Talbert and Gothard Street, on the far eastern side of the park. The ride is on the west side of the park, so head south on Gothard. Turn right on Ellis Avenue. At Edwards Street, turn right, with the park now on your right. Turn right on Inlet Drive, and then enter the park on the right. Route 76 runs every hour on weekdays (no service on weekends or holidays).

Starting point coordinates: 33.698272°N / 118.014692°W

The Ride

Central Park Discs and Dobbins is a short (3.4-mile) off-road ride with plenty of variety. The ride title refers to a disc golf course that the route passes and a network of shared trails

WINTERSBURG

Located 2 miles to the northeast of Central Park is Wintersburg, in Huntington Beach. The site was a locus of Japanese immigration from the late nineteenth century until the early 2000s. The Issei, or first-generation Japanese immigrants, started landing in California around 1885, mainly in San Francisco. By 1908, Japanese immigrants had pioneered their way southward to Wintersburg, where they established a Presbyterian mission and small village. The mission was part of a Japanese Mission Trail that was similar to the Spanish Mission Trail established in California during the nineteenth century; the Japanese version has never been fully recognized. During World War II, Wintersburg's landowners and residents were sent to detention camps, along with thousands of other Japanese. When the landowners finally returned to Wintersburg, the site was in disrepair. After a long period of rebuilding, the Furuta family's flower farm grew to become the largest American supplier of cut water lilies. The Furutas finally abandoned Wintersburg in 2004, as no one in the family was farming and others had long deserted the village. The site still features six buildings, including the original Japanese Presbyterian mission, built in 1910. There are no formal tours, or even signage, but a visit to Wintersburg may be worthwhile. Wintersburg is located to the north of Warner Avenue, east of Gothard Street.

adjacent an equestrian center that is home to a number of "dobbins." Only a few of the paths and trails in Huntington Beach's Central Park have markers. Half of the ride tours the western portion of the park (the route does not visit the eastern portion). The other half of the ride tours an equestrian trails area, immediately adjacent to the park, that is suitable for mountain biking. Be sure to give way to horses when bicycling the trails.

Miles and Directions

0.0 Start adjacent to Dog Park in Central Park; exit parking lot toward the south, riding onto paved path.

0.15 End of paved path—continue onto dirt trail (watch for tree roots).

0.35 Paved path resumes; path curves left to remain lakeside, and then right.

0.5 Path leaves lake area.

0.6 Stay left at fork.

0.65 Stay right, and continue curving right, on paved path.

0.8 Turn left onto dirt trail.

0.85 End of trail; right onto walkway.

0.95 Right onto trail, leaving walkway (re-enter park).

1.1 Bear left, re-merging with paved path.

1.2 Veer left, leaving path, riding onto trail—trail climbs hillside to disc golf area.

1.35 Enter disc golf area; stay on periphery, riding along the edge.

1.45 Leave golf area; turn 180° to right and return along opposite side of wooden fence.

1.65 Descend from frisbee area, along trail adjacent to equestrian facilities.

1.85 Left to enter equestrian trails area—begin short (200 feet) climb (13.3% grade).

1.9 Bear left at top of climb.

1.95 Stay right; equestrian facilities at left.

2.0 Curve left; short climb (5.0% grade).

2.1 Stay left at fork.

2.35 Right onto rudimentary trail to cross open space.

2.4 Bear right—aim toward shallow canyon ahead; trail curves right to parallel the wash, then left to cross it.

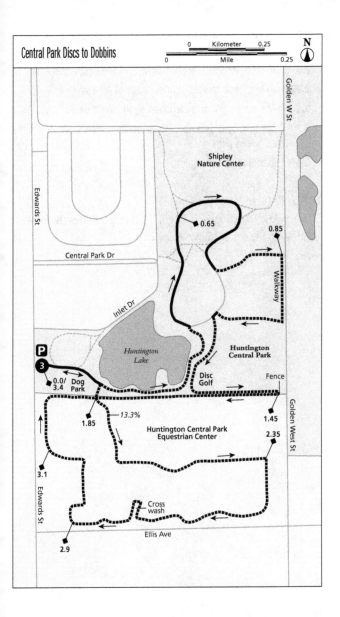

Central Park Discs to Dobbins

0   Kilometer   0.25
0   Mile   0.25

N

Golden W St

Shipley
Nature Center

0.65

0.85

Edwards St

Central Park Dr

Walkway

Huntington
Central Park

Inlet Dr

Huntington
Lake

P
3

0.0/
3.4

Dog
Park

Disc
Golf

Fence

1.45

13.3%

2.35

Golden West St

1.85

Huntington Central Park
Equestrian Center

3.1

Edwards St

Cross
wash

Ellis Ave

2.9

2.7 After crossing the wash, trail makes short climb, curving left—continue as trail curves right (Peppertree Trail).

2.9 Turn right, followed by another right (leave Peppertree Trail).

2.95 Turn left; head toward northern edge of equestrian area.

3.1 Trail curves right, and then right again, while descending.

3.3 Equestrian area gateway; left to return to main park, then left onto paved path.

3.4 End of ride at parking lot.

BIKE SHOP

HB Cycles, 19729 Beach Blvd., Huntington Beach, (714) 594–3844, www.hbcyclesusa.com

4 Costa Mesa Cruise

Start: Tanager Park, 1780 Hummingbird Drive, Costa Mesa
Length: 4.25 miles (clockwise loop, with zigs and zags in Fairview Park)
Riding time: 20 to 50 minutes (my time: 38:31 on foot)
Terrain and surface: 38% graded dirt trails, 35% paved bike paths, 17% paved roads, and 10% concrete walkway
Elevations: Low—11 feet on Placentia Avenue walkway, north side of Fairview Park; high—73 feet along bike path on south side of Costa Mesa Golf Course
Traffic and hazards: Placentia Avenue carried 11,000 vehicles daily adjacent to Fairview Park.
Map: *The Thomas Guide by Rand McNally—Street Guide: Los Angeles and Orange Counties* (any recent year), page 858
Getting there by car: From central Anaheim, head south on I-5 (or south on CA 57 to I-5). Exit to CA 55 freeway southbound. Exit to I-405 northbound. Exit at Harbor Boulevard (in Costa Mesa) and head south. Right on Adams Avenue, then left on Mesa Verde Drive East. Right on Golf Course Drive, then right on Tanager Drive. Look for Tanager Park on the right; park on street.
Getting there by public transit: OCTA bus route 47 runs between Fullerton and Newport Beach along multiple roads. Exit bus at Harbor Boulevard and Adams Avenue in Costa Mesa; head west on Adams. Orange Coast College will be at left. Turn left on Mesa Verde Drive East. Right on Golf Course Drive, then right on Tanager Drive. Tanager Park will be on the right. Route 47 runs every 20 minutes on weekdays and every 30 minutes on weekends and holidays.
Starting point coordinates: 33.669014°N / 117.929536°W

The Ride

The Costa Mesa Cruise is a 4.25-mile, mostly off-road, clockwise loop in southwest Costa Mesa. The ride uses trails on the lightly developed east side of Fairview Park, on one side of the route's loop, and a series of paved bike paths on the other side, to complete the loop. The east side of Fairview Park has a few crisscrossing trails and some railroad track. The Orange County Model Engineers (OCME) have built 5 miles of just over one-eighth scale railroad there (please see sidebar). You could complete this ride on a mountain, hybrid, or cyclocross bike. The entire ride is within the city of Costa Mesa, which had an estimated population of 113,615 in 2018. Costa Mesa is home to the annual Orange

MODEL RAILROADING IN COSTA MESA

When riding around Fairview Park's lightly developed east side, you will notice some narrow-gauge railroad track crossings. Has the park been invaded by a Lilliputian contingency? No—the tracks are the work of Orange County Model Engineers (OCME). The group was formed in 1977, after the similar Long Beach Live Steamers went defunct. After several years of negotiations, the OCME secured 40 acres of land on their current site, in 1989. Construction began on 600 feet of track. By 1998, another 4,200 feet had been added. Their Mackerel Flats & Goat Hill Junction Station was constructed in 1999. More track was completed by 2003. Some of the work required transplantation of native purple needlegrass, an endangered plant that was growing along the rights-of-way. There are now 5 miles of track, including sidings, wyes, and dual-track segments. The gauge is 7.5 inches, which is slightly larger than one-eighth scale. The OCME equipment includes six engines and forty-five "bench" cars, which are suitable for passengers. The cars are simple, open-air vehicles. The OCME work is very precise, as is needed to build and operate a successful rail facility. A train ride, which was free as of this writing and available on the third weekend of every month, is highly recommended.

County Fair, El Pollo Loco, Toyota Racing Development, Vanguard University, and skateboard clothing maker Vans. After entering the eastern side of Fairview Park, at mile 2.35, the ride makes maximum use of the trail network. There are a few zigs and zags! None of the trails is named or marked, so please be sure to study the map, as well as the "Miles and Directions." Exercise caution when crossing the OCME railroad track, as there are no signals or barriers.

Miles and Directions

0.0 Start at Tanager Park in Costa Mesa; head east from Hummingbird Drive on Tanager Drive.

0.15 Stop sign at Golf Course Drive; keep straight, veering slightly right, onto paved path.

0.45 At-grade crossing of Harla Avenue.

0.6 End of path at Harbor Boulevard; right onto walkway.

0.65 Cross Merrimac Way (traffic signal)—continue on walkway, adjacent to Harbor Boulevard.

1.0 Keep straight at Fair Drive (traffic signal)—after crossing, veer right onto parallel bike path.

1.3 Path curves right; Costa Mesa Golf Course at right.

1.9 Highest elevation of ride: 73 feet.

2.05 End of path; right onto Placentia Avenue.

2.35 Leave Placentia Avenue; right into driveway (dirt)—aim for OCME train station.

2.45 Ride past station, onto graded dirt trail—cross railroad tracks with caution.

2.6 Left on concrete walkway.

2.7 Cross railroad tracks.

2.75 Right onto dirt trail.

2.85 Right on concrete walkway.

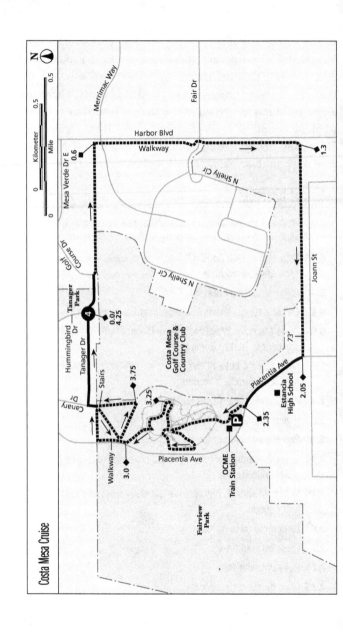

Costa Mesa Cruise

2.9 Cross railroad tracks again, left onto graded dirt trail.

2.95 Straight at next two trail junctions.

3.0 Trail makes a sweeping U-turn to left.

3.05 Straight at merge, then stay left at next merge.

3.15 Right on trail—cross two railroad tracks and begin descent (12.2% grade).

3.25 End of descent; right onto walkway adjacent to Placentia Avenue.

3.35 At the edge of open space (lowest elevation of ride: 11 feet), right to climb hill (9.3% grade).

3.45 Top of hill; turn sharply right—cut diagonally across open space (descent: 6.8% grade).

3.6 End of descent; turn sharply left; ride trail adjacent to channel (gradual climb).

3.75 Left on trail, eastern edge of open space (Costa Mesa Golf Course at right)—gradual climb (4% grade).

3.9 Top of climb, at trail junction—bear right to leave park; walk down short staircase, continue via Canary Drive.

3.95 Right on Tanager Drive.

4.25 End ride at Hummingbird Drive, adjacent to Tanager Park.

BIKE SHOPS

Barcelo Bicycles, 130 E. 17th St., Costa Mesa, (949) 722–7002, http://barcelo-bicycles.business.site

The Cyclist Bike Shop, 1785 Newport Blvd., Costa Mesa, (949) 645–8691, www.thecyclist.com

5 Fullerton Pump & Circumstance

Start: Hillcrest Park, 1200 North Harbor Boulevard, Fullerton
Length: 6.8 miles (lollipop with long counterclockwise loop)
Riding time: 25 to 75 minutes (my time: 32:23)
Terrain and surface: 80% paved roads and 20% concrete bike paths
Elevations: Low–158 feet at Berkeley and Wilshire Avenues; high–252 feet at Hillcrest Park (staging point)
Traffic and hazards: Daily traffic volumes were 25,000 on Yorba Linda Boulevard north of California State University, Fullerton; 18,000 on Commonwealth Avenue west of State College Boulevard; 10,000 on Commonwealth east of State College; and 9,000 on Berkeley Avenue adjacent to Fullerton College. Yorba Linda Boulevard adjacent CSU Fullerton has no shoulder–use walkway.
Map: *The Thomas Guide by Rand McNally—Street Guide: Los Angeles and Orange Counties* (any recent year), page 738
Getting there by car: From central Anaheim, head north on Harbor Boulevard, entering Fullerton. Turn right on Valley View Drive to head east; Hillcrest Park is on the left. Left to enter park, prior to arriving at Lemon Street.
Getting there by public transit: OCTA bus route 43 travels along Harbor Boulevard between Fullerton and Costa Mesa. The route terminates at Fullerton Station, 1 mile south of Hillcrest Park. OCTA bus route 143 continues along Harbor, passing by the park. Route 43 runs every 20 minutes on weekdays and every 25 minutes on weekends and holidays. Route 143 runs every 65 to 75 minutes daily. Alternatively, three Metrolink lines serve Fullerton Station. All three lines begin at Union Station in central Los Angeles; the OC and Surfliner trains continue to San Diego, while Riverside trains continue to San Bernardino. There are forty trains in each direction on weekdays and twenty-three in each direction on weekends. Transfer to route 143, or ride to Hillcrest Park via Lemon Street.
Starting point coordinates: 33.881258°N / 117.920311°W

The Ride

Fullerton Pump & Circumstance is a fun urban ride through the city of Fullerton. The 6.8-mile road ride includes a 6.4-mile counterclockwise loop, plus a 0.2-mile starting and ending out-and-back segment. The elevation differential is 94 feet. The ride cuts through the California State University, Fullerton (CSUF) campus and uses a bike path along Fullerton Creek. The ride starts and ends at Hillcrest Park. The park opened in 1922 and is on the National Register of Historic Places (NRHP). Its features include the Izaak Walton Cabin, the Red Cross Building, and the Works Progress Administration fountain and surrounding stonework. Many folks come here to climb a seven-flight staircase that was completed in

CALIFORNIA STATE UNIVERSITY, FULLERTON

"Fullerton Pump & Circumstance" is unusual in that it penetrates the campus of California State University, Fullerton. A marked bikeway through campus encourages you to ride. Exercise caution and "slow your roll," as the campus can be busy with students and other users. CSUF's enrollment of 39,770 students, as of Fall 2018, made it the largest in the twenty-three-school California State University System. CSUF was founded in 1957, placing it in the middle of the state system's older and newer universities. Notable CSUF graduates include actor-director Kevin Costner, astronaut Tracy Caldwell Dyson, Congressman Ed Royce, news anchor Michelle Ruiz, pop songstress Gwen Stefani, and many others. As for sports, CSUF competes In NCAA Division I. The school's baseball team has won four NCAA championships and trained numerous players who advanced to Major League Baseball. The school has also won three men's and three women's NCAA gymnastics titles. And the CSUF jazz dance team has won a whopping fifteen(!) national titles.

2017. The long staircase is on the northwest side of the park, if you are game (the ride stages on the southeast side). The route passes Fullerton College, which is a two-year community college. The college has an independent look and was established in 1913, long before the California community college system existed. Notable alumni include pro footballer Kevin McLain, film director James Cameron, actor-producer-director William Conrad, and First Lady Patricia Nixon. On the CSUF campus, with nearly 40,000 students, be sure to check your speed. When I tested this ride, a faint line on the ground marked the bike route, but it was admittedly hard to see in some locations. There is also signing, but these were also difficult to follow, particularly while observing other path users. Please be sure to study the map and the "Miles and Directions." The ride passes Fullerton Arboretum, a 26-acre botanical garden on the CSUF campus. It is the largest in Orange County, and Heritage House, on the grounds of the arboretum, is on the NRHP.

Miles and Directions

0.0 Start in Hillcrest Park in Fullerton, on Valley View Drive side of park (highest elevation of ride: 252 feet); turn left and enter Valley View.

0.05 Stop sign at Lemon Street—turn right (downhill, 6.5% grade).

0.2 Traffic signal at Berkeley Avenue—turn left.

0.45 Traffic signal at Hornet Way—keep straight (return here later).

0.65 Berkeley Avenue curves right; Fullerton College athletic fields at right.

0.85 Traffic signal at Chapman Avenue—keep straight; road narrows.

1.0 Stop sign at Wilshire Avenue—turn left (lowest elevation of ride: 158 feet).

1.15 Stop sign at Lincoln Avenue and at Raymond Avenue (mile 1.4)—keep straight.

1.9 Stop sign at Acacia Avenue—turn right.

2.05 Traffic signal at Commonwealth Avenue—turn left.

2.40 Traffic signal at Little Avenue, adjacent school, and at State College Boulevard (mile 2.55)—keep straight.

2.65 Commonwealth Avenue curves left to head north.

3.0 Traffic signal at Chapman Avenue—keep straight; enter Cal State Fullerton environs.

3.25 Traffic signal at Nutwood Avenue (end of Commonwealth)—cross Nutwood; right on campus bike path.

3.35 Follow path as it travels between campus buildings on left and parking facilities at right.

3.6 Stay right at split in path—Engineering and Computer Science quad (grassy area) at left.

3.7 Stay left at fork—Student Health and Counseling building at left.

3.75 Cross campus road; Titan House (athletics administration) at left.

4.0 Path curves left.

4.05 Leave path to the right; enter North Campus Drive to head north.

4.15 Traffic signal at Yorba Linda Boulevard; turn left to ride on walkway.

4.4 Traffic signal at State College Boulevard—keep straight.

4.45 Bear left onto concrete bike path, adjacent to Fullerton Creek (elevation: 250 feet).

4.7 Stay left at all junctions (but do not cross bridge over Fullerton Creek).

4.95 Bear left at merger.

5.05 End path at Melody Lane—continue into road.

5.15 Stop sign at Acacia Avenue (end of Melody)—turn left.

Fullerton Pump & Circumstance

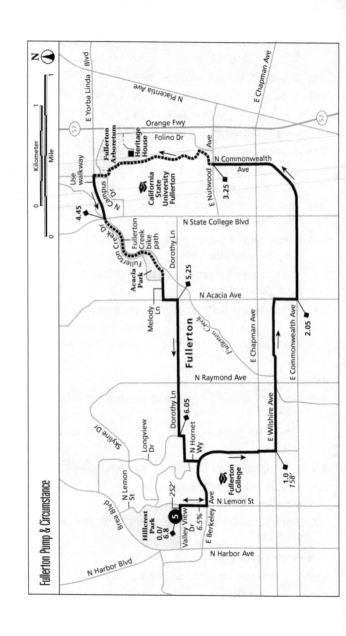

5.25 Stop sign at Dorothy Lane—turn right.

5.75 Stop sign at Raymond Avenue—keep straight.

6.05 Stop sign at Longview Street—turn left, continue on Dorothy.

6.1 Dorothy Lane curves right.

6.25 Dorothy curves left to become Hornet Way.

6.35 Traffic signal at Berkeley Avenue—turn right.

6.6 Traffic signal at Lemon Street—turn right; begin climb (6.5% grade).

6.75 Turn left on Valley View Drive—continue climbing (11.4% grade).

6.8 End ride at Hillcrest Park.

BIKE SHOPS

East West Bikes, 206 N. Harbor Blvd., Fullerton, (714) 525–2200, www.ewbikes.com

Fullerton Bicycles, 424 E. Commonwealth Ave., Fullerton, (714) 879–8310, www.fullertonbicycle.com

6 Mile Square Squall

Start: Mile Square Regional Park, 16582 Brookhurst Street (Boys & Girls Club: Kingston Branch), Fountain Valley
Length: 5.45 miles (clockwise loop)
Riding time: 20 to 50 minutes (my time: 24:48)
Terrain and surface: 71% concrete paths, 15% graded dirt paths, and 14% paved roads
Elevations: Low—27 feet on the west side of Mile Square Regional Park; high—45 feet at the northeast corner of Mile Square Regional Park
Traffic and hazards: 100% park paths and roads. Pathways on the north side of the park are heavily used and crossed by park users.
Map: *The Thomas Guide by Rand McNally—Street Guide: Los Angeles and Orange Counties* (any recent year), page 828

Getting there by car: From central Anaheim, head south on I-5. Exit to CA 55 freeway and head south. Exit to I-405 northbound. Exit at Brookhurst Street, in Fountain Valley, and turn right. After passing Warner Avenue, Mile Square Regional Park is at right; enter at the Boys & Girls Club building.
Getting there by public transit: OCTA bus route 35 runs along Brookhurst Street between Fullerton and Costa Mesa, along the western border of Mile Square Regional Park. Exit bus at Boys & Girls Club building. Route 35 runs every 40 minutes on weekdays and every 45 to 50 minutes on weekends and holidays.
Starting point coordinates: 33.722011°N / 117.953964°W

The Ride

Mile Square Squall is the most compact road ride in the book, staying entirely within Fountain Valley's Mile Square Regional Park. The park literally covers 1 square mile—1 mile long on each of the park's four sides. With a couple of

FOUNTAIN VALLEY

Fountain Valley is a predominantly residential city in west-central Orange County. The estimated population was 55,810 in 2018, having changed little since 1980. A stable population is unusual for Orange County cities, most of which have been experiencing growth. Fountain Valley is the headquarters of Hyundai Motors America and SureFire (flashlights), among others. Notable graduates of Fountain Valley's three high schools include author and screenwriter Kim Gruenenfelder; Major League Baseball pitchers Luke Hudson, Casey Janssen, and C. J. Wilson; NFL (USA) player and NFL (Europe) coach Ken Margerum; actress Michelle Pfeiffer; Secretary of State Mike Pompeo; and actor Brian Van Holt. Population growth in the city around 1980 was heavily oriented toward an influx of Vietnamese immigrants, after the Vietnam War. As of 2010, the heritage of one-third of the city's population was Asian.

segments into the interior of the park, the total length is 5.45 miles. The elevation differential is 18 feet. The opening 0.85 miles are on graded dirt paths that are suitable for a road bike. The rest of the ride is on concrete and pavement. The park features two golf courses and Mile Square Park Lake, all of which the ride passes. The north side of the park tends to be busier than the south side, particularly near the lake. You may see a few rented quad-cycles, one of the offbeat activities available to enjoy.

Miles and Directions

0.0 Start on the south side of Boys & Girls Club: Kingston Branch parking lot at Mile Square Regional Park in Fountain Valley; head into the park via graded dirt path.

0.5 Stay right at fork.

0.55 Path curves left (baseball fields at left; Mile Square Golf Course at right).

0.7 Path curves left (and at mile 0.8).

0.85 Leave path; veer right, enter park road.

0.9 Park road curves right—David L. Baker Memorial Golf Course at right.

1.15 End of park road at Brookhurst Street—right onto concrete path.

1.35 Northwest corner of Mile Square Regional Park—right to continue on path (Edinger Avenue at left).

1.8 Traffic signal at park entrance—keep straight on concrete path.

2.1 Bear left adjacent to Mile Square Park Lake.

2.15 Path curves left, heading toward bordering road (Edinger Avenue).

2.35 Northeast corner of Mile Square Regional Park (highest elevation of ride: 45 feet)—right to continue on path (Euclid Street at left).

2.65 Right on path at park entrance opposite Blue Allium Avenue.

2.7 Path curves right.

2.75 Left at path junction, and then left onto park road.

2.9 Right onto parking access road.

2.95 At crosswalk, left onto concrete path—path curves right and then left (baseball fields at left; Mile Square Golf Course at right).

3.45 Path curves left, crosses bridge.

3.5 Right at T junction—make counterclockwise loop of large grass field.

3.7 Leave path by veering right; enter parking access road and turn left.

3.8 End of parking access road—right onto park road.

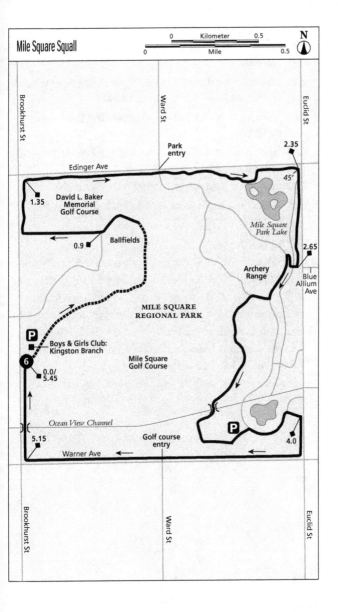

Mile Square Squall

0 Kilometer 0.5
0 Mile 0.5

N

Brookhurst St
Ward St
Euclid St

Park entry

2.35

Edinger Ave

1.35

David L. Baker Memorial Golf Course

45'

0.9 Ballfields

Mile Square Park Lake

MILE SQUARE REGIONAL PARK

Archery Range

2.65

Blue Allium Ave

P

Boys & Girls Club: Kingston Branch

6

0.0/ 5.45

Mile Square Golf Course

Ocean View Channel

5.15

P

4.0

Warner Ave

Golf course entry

Brookhurst St
Ward St
Euclid St

3.95 Bear right, head toward park exit.

4.0 End of park exit road at Euclid Street; right onto concrete walkway.

4.15 Southeast corner of Mile Square Regional Park—right to continue on walkway (Warner Avenue at left).

4.65 Traffic signal at entrance to Mile Square Golf Course—keep straight.

5.15 Southwest corner of Mile Square Regional Park—right to continue on walkway (Brookhurst Street at left).

5.25 Bear right to continue on concrete path—path crosses bridge.

5.45 Return to parking area for Boys & Girls Club—end of ride.

BIKE SHOPS

Bicycle Discovery, 8800 Warner Ave., Warner Plaza, Fountain Valley, (714) 841–1366, www.bicycle-discovery.com

Epic Ride Shop (BMX bike shop), 16483 Magnolia St., Westminster, (714) 848–0888, www.epicbmx.com

Wheel Fun Rentals (bike rentals), 16801 Euclid St. (two locations within Mile Square Regional Park), Fountain Valley, (714) 719–0384 or (714) 719–1032, http://wheelfunrentals.com

7 Plateau Placentia

Start: Park at La Jolla and Gonzales Streets in southwestern Placentia

Length: 10.65 miles (figure eight plus short out-and-back)

Riding time: 30 to 100 minutes (my time: 43:34)

Terrain and surface: 100% paved roads

Elevations: Low—198 feet at La Jolla and Gonzales Streets; high—415 feet at Wabash Avenue and Prospect Avenue.

Traffic and hazards: Daily traffic volumes were 23,000 on Kraemer Boulevard south of Orangethorpe Avenue, 13,000 on Orangethorpe between Kraemer and Rose Drive, 31,000 on Rose Drive at Buena Vista Avenue, and 20,000 on Bastanchury Road east of Kraemer. Use caution where Kraemer passes under Crowther Avenue.

Map: *The Thomas Guide by Rand McNally—Street Guide: Los Angeles and Orange Counties* (any recent year), page 769

Getting there by car: From central Anaheim, head north on CA 57. Exit at Orangethorpe Avenue, in Placentia, and turn right. Turn right on Melrose Street and head south. Right at La Jolla Street; stay right where road splits. Enter neighborhood—unnamed park is straight ahead; park on street.

Getting there by public transit: OCTA bus route 30 runs along Orangethorpe Avenue between northeastern Anaheim and Cerritos, passing through Placentia. Exit bus at Melrose Street and head south. Turn right on La Jolla Street, and keep straight to the park. Route 30 runs every 30 minutes on weekdays and every 65 minutes on weekends and holidays.

Starting point coordinates: 33.857944°N / 117.875433°W

The Ride

Plateau Placentia is designed according to the objective of riding from a city's lowest to its highest elevation and then

PLACENTIA

Settlement of Placentia began as early as the late 1830s, on land that was granted to Juan Pacifico Ontiveros by the governor of Mexico. In 1865, Daniel Kraemer purchased much of Ontiveros's holdings, and an influx of settlers began. The first commercial Valencia orange grove in Orange County was planted in Placentia in 1880, by Richard Gilman. By then, the community already had its name, although the origin is unknown. Agriculture was at the root of the community's first population surge. Oil was discovered in Placentia in 1919, leading to a second population surge. Placentia incorporated in 1926. As Orange County grew during the twentieth century, large orange groves were transformed into residential communities. The transformation process continues today, although the city still has a few scattered groves. Population growth in the city was most dramatic between 1950 and 1970, when it grew by a factor of ten, to 21,950. The population doubled again by 1990, to 41,260. Since then, growth has been at an average rate of 0.8% per year. The composition of the populace has shifted from a Caucasian majority; by 2010 Hispanics (36%) and Asian Americans (14%) represented half of the city's residents.

returning. The plan works well for some cities, but not for all. Such a ride for Los Angeles could take more than a day, climbing over 5,000 feet in 70 miles and then returning. Plateau Placentia is comparatively tiny and compact, climbing from 198 feet at the starting point to 415 feet in the city's northeast corner and then returning. The route "cheats" by leaving Placentia to pass through Yorba Linda. Placentia's highest elevation is 404 feet, at Rose Drive and Wabash Avenue; the ride enters Yorba Linda, continuing to 415 feet. There are no steep or extended climbs, but you will notice some gradual elevation changes. The route uses designated bike routes and roads with bike lanes, with a few discontinuities and plenty of traffic signals along the way. The total distance is 10.65 miles, which comprises an 8.45-mile figure eight, plus a 1.1-mile out-and-back segment. The start and finish are at an unnamed neighborhood park located at the corner of La Jolla and Gonzales Streets, in extreme southwest Placentia. Placentia had a slowly growing population of 51,670 in 2018. Along Orangethorpe Avenue, the ride passes Anaheim Lake (mile 1.6), a fishing lake that was closed as of this writing. On Kraemer Boulevard just north of Yorba Linda Boulevard (mile 7.9), on the right, is Bradford Park, which is home to the A. S. Bradford House. The house is on the National Register of Historic Places, built in 1902. Albert Sumner Bradford is credited with bringing the railroad to Placentia and with laying out the city's street pattern. On Kraemer, on the approach to Alta Vista Street (mile 8.75), at right is Valencia High School. Famous graduates include three-time tennis Grand Slam runner-up Michael Chang, 1996 Olympic softball gold medalist Michelle Granger, Congresswoman Linda Sanchez, and Olympic water polo (2000) and triathlon (2008) team member Julie Swail!

Miles and Directions

- **0.0** Start at unnamed park adjacent to La Jolla and Gonzales Streets; head east on La Jolla.
- **0.05** Stop sign at Tafolla Street, traffic signal at Melrose Street (mile 0.1), and stop sign at Red Gum Street (mile 0.45)—keep straight on La Jolla at each intersection.
- **0.85** Traffic signal at Kraemer Boulevard—turn left.
- **1.1** Traffic signal at Orangethorpe Avenue—turn right; begin figure eight.
- **1.6** Begin overpass—Orangethorpe climbs gradually.

1.7 Traffic signal at Miller Street, at Chapman Avenue (mile 1.95), and at Traub Lane (mile 2.05)—keep straight on Orangethorpe at each intersection.

2.25 Orangethorpe passes under Rose Drive.

2.3 Traffic signal at connector to Rose Drive—turn left; climb 5.0% grade.

2.4 Traffic signal at Rose Drive (end of connector)—turn right.

2.6 Traffic signal at Castner Drive and at Alta Vista Street (mile 2.85), Buena Vista Avenue (mile 3.15), Palm Drive (mile 3.3), Valparaiso Way (mile 3.5), Yorba Linda Boulevard (mile 3.75; enter Yorba Linda), Bastanchury Road (mile 4.5), and Imperial Highway (mile 4.85; re-enter Placentia)—keep straight on Rose at each intersection.

5.0 Traffic signal at Wabash Avenue; turn right—highest elevation in Placentia (404 feet); re-enter Yorba Linda.

5.3 Wabash Avenue ends—continue on adjacent path; highest elevation of ride (415 feet).

5.35 Re-enter roadway; right on Prospect Avenue.

5.55 Traffic signal at CA 90—keep straight.

5.8 Traffic signal at Bastanchury Road—turn right.

5.95 Traffic signal at Grey Stone Drive and at Rose Drive (mile 6.0), McCormack Lane (mile 6.4; re-enter Placentia), Valencia Avenue (mile 6.8), and Brookhaven Avenue (mile 7.05)—keep straight on Bastanchury at each intersection.

7.35 Traffic signal at Kraemer Boulevard—turn left on Kraemer.

7.9 Traffic signal at Yorba Linda Boulevard—keep straight on Kraemer; Bradford Park and A. S. Bradford House are on the right.

8.1 Traffic signal at Sheffield Street and at Madison Avenue (mile 8.45), Alta Vista Street (mile 8.75), Chapman Avenue (mile 9.1), and Hawaii Way (mile 9.2)—keep straight on Kraemer at each intersection.

9.3 Kraemer passes under Crowther Avenue.

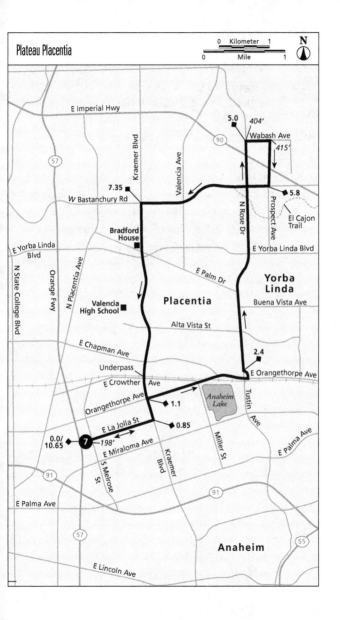

Plateau Placentia

9.55 Traffic signal at Orangethorpe Avenue—keep straight; end of figure eight.

9.8 Traffic signal at La Jolla Street—turn right.

10.2 Stop sign at Red Gum Street, traffic signal at Melrose Street (mile 10.55), and stop sign at Tafolla Street (mile 10.6)—keep straight on La Jolla at each intersection.

10.65 End of ride at Gonzales Street, adjacent to park.

BIKE SHOPS

BikeCraze (bicycles and electric bikes), 1171 N. Kraemer Blvd., Anaheim, (714) 744–0266, www.bikecraze.com

Duke's Bicycles, 1401 S. Kraemer Blvd., Anaheim, (714) 869–8818, www.dukesbicycles.com

8 Santiago Hills, Oaks & Spokes

Start: Santiago Hills Park, 8040 East White Oak Ridge, Orange
Length: 5.75 miles (clockwise loop)
Riding time: 30 to 75 minutes (my time: 59:41 on foot)
Terrain and surface: 63% dirt trails, 23% concrete paths, and 14% paved roads
Elevations: Low—484 feet on Kennymead Street at Wilderness Avenue in Orange; high—634 feet near the Coachwhip Trail-Barham Ridge Trail junction
Traffic and hazards: Santiago Canyon Road carried 29,000 vehicles per day near Santiago Oaks Regional Park. Use caution when turning left from Santiago Canyon onto Lolita Street.
Map: *The Thomas Guide by Rand McNally—Street Guide: Los Angeles and Orange Counties* (any recent year), page 800

Getting there by car: From central Anaheim, head east on Katella Avenue. Katella becomes Villa Park Road in Villa Park, and then Santiago Canyon Road in Orange. Right on Newport Road to head south. Left on White Oak Ridge to head east. Santiago Hills Park is at right. Turn right on Trail's End Road to enter the park.
Getting there by public transit: OCTA bus route 54 runs between Garden Grove and Santiago Canyon College in Orange via Chapman Avenue. Exit the bus at Trail's End Road, opposite Santiago Canyon College, and head south. Santiago Hills Park is straight ahead. Route 54 runs every 20 minutes on weekdays and every 30 minutes on weekends and holidays.
Starting point coordinates: 33.791936°N / 117.767669°W

The Ride

Santiago Hills, Oaks & Spokes admittedly pushes the boundaries of "easy." The elevation differential is just 150 feet, but there is triple that amount of climbing in between the high and low elevations. There are three short (each 250 feet long) climbs.

ORANGE PARK ACRES

The city of Orange is unique in Orange County in that it completely surrounds several communities that are not part of Orange. These include El Modena, Orange Park Acres, and the city of Villa Park. Orange Park Acres is in the northeast quadrant of Orange, east of Villa Park. The community had a population of 5,500 in 2010. The ride does not enter Orange Park Acres, but the route makes a turn on the edge of the community (at Kennymead Street). In 1928, Orange Park Acres was founded as Orange County's official equestrian destination. Since then, the community has resisted the installation of sidewalks and streetlights, preferring its network of paved roads and equestrian trails. Long before mountain bikes debuted, and even after, many trails have been developed as a result of equestrian advocacy. Although the route does not enter Orange Park Acres, the horse trails that the ride uses may be an outgrowth of the community's efforts. Be sure to give way to any horseback riders when traveling along the trails.

There are some fun downhills, too, allowing you to recover, as well as some false flats. This mountain bike ride is a 5.75-mile clockwise loop in northeastern Orange. The ride stages at Santiago Hills Park and uses equestrian trails and a few roads to arrive at Santiago Oaks Regional Park. Be cautious and respectful of equestrians on the trails. The ride continues along county-owned trails, entering and then leaving Irvine Regional Park to continue along the bike path adjacent to Jamboree Road. Santiago Canyon College's Coastkeeper Garden is adjacent to Jamboree, just outside of Irvine Regional Park. (The garden is open Wednesday through Saturday and is worth a visit.) Beyond Jamboree, the ride uses a roadside trail along Canyon View Avenue to return to the south side of Santiago Hills Park. The park is a popular staging point for cyclists. Parking is free, and there is an abundance of trails and road routes nearby.

Miles and Directions

0.0 Start on northwest side of Santiago Hills Park in Orange, on concrete path; head north.

0.05 Cross White Oak Ridge (paved road; no controls).

0.25 Bear right upon approaching Chapman Avenue.

0.3 End of path; left onto Chapman Avenue's walkway—at intersection of Chapman and Newport Boulevard, cross one street and then the other.

0.35 From the opposite corner of Chapman and Newport, head north on the equestrian trail, parallel to Newport (4.8% grade).

0.7 Trail curves left—now descending, parallel to Santiago Canyon Road.

0.85 Trail curves left to cross Lakeview Trail (paved road); start short climb (17.4% grade).

0.9 Crest of climb; begin descent (19.3% grade).

0.95 End of descent; begin climb (18.9% grade).

1.0 Crest of climb—highest elevation of ride (634 feet).

1.1 Turn sharply to right to continue on equestrian trail.

1.15 Begin short climb (16.4% grade).

1.2 Cross Amapola Avenue (no controls) and then Ridgeline Road (no controls)—begin long descent on trail.

1.6 Keep straight at trail junction.

1.9 End of trail; right onto Kennymead Street (paved road).

2.05 Lowest elevation of ride (484 feet), at Wilderness Avenue.

2.15 End of street; lift bike over curb and turn right to ride on shoulder of Santiago Canyon Road (5.5% grade).

2.4 Turn left on Lolita Street—use caution in crossing Santiago Canyon's lanes.

2.5 End of Lolita—enter Santiago Oaks Regional Park; paved road continues to top of Villa Park Dam (5.3% grade).

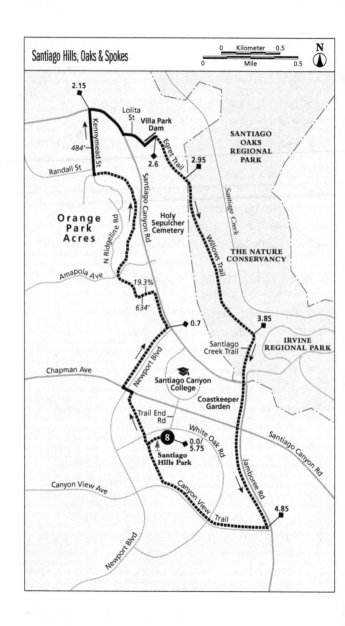

Santiago Hills, Oaks & Spokes

N

0   Kilometer   0.5

0   Mile   0.5

2.15

Lolita St

Villa Park Dam

Kennymead St

484'

Randall St

SANTIAGO OAKS REGIONAL PARK

Egret Trail

2.6

2.95

Santiago Creek

Orange Park Acres

N Ridgeline Rd

Santiago Canyon Rd

Holy Sepulcher Cemetery

THE NATURE CONSERVANCY

Willows Trail

Amapola Ave

19.3%

634'

0.7

3.85

IRVINE REGIONAL PARK

Santiago Creek Trail

Chapman Ave

Newport Blvd

Santiago Canyon College

Coastkeeper Garden

Trail End Rd

8

0.0/5.75

Santiago Hills Park

White Oak Rd

Santiago Canyon Rd

Canyon View Ave

Canyon View Trail

Jamboree Rd

4.85

Newport Blvd

2.6 At crest of dam, turn right onto dirt trail—go around gate and descend into basin (11.4% grade).

2.65 Keep right at bottom of downhill.

2.7 Bear left onto Egret Trail.

2.95 Left at trail junction onto Willows Trail; continue across basin—enter Irvine Regional Park.

3.85 Right on Santiago Creek Trail (wide track with loose rocks)—gradual climb.

4.0 Keep straight as trail exits Irvine Regional Park—now parallel to Jamboree Road.

4.1 Traffic signal at Santiago Canyon Road—keep straight; continue onto concrete bike path.

4.2 Coastkeeper Garden at right; begin gradual descent.

4.3 Traffic signal at Chapman Avenue and at Fort Road (mile 4.5)—keep straight on bike path.

4.85 Traffic signal at Canyon View Avenue—cross Canyon View and turn right on Canyon View Equestrian Trail.

5.0 Peters Canyon Regional Park at left—keep straight.

5.2 Traffic signal at White Oak Ridge—keep straight.

5.5 Traffic signal at Aspen (paved road)—cross Aspen and then Canyon View; continue onto concrete path to enter Santiago Hills Park.

5.75 End of ride at path junction, adjacent to ballfields.

BIKE SHOPS

Adrenaline Bike Shop, 366 S. Tustin St., Orange, (714) 288–2012, www.adrenalinebikes.com

Bike Alley (BMX specialist), 2823 E. Chapman Ave., Orange, (714) 997–3980, http://bikealleybmx.com

9 Upper Irvine-Northwood Nexus

Start: Harvard Community Park, 14701 Harvard Avenue, Irvine
Length: 14.8 miles (clockwise loop)
Riding time: 45 to 135 minutes (my time: 58:23)
Terrain and surface: 73% paved bike paths, 25% paved roads, and 2% concrete walkways
Elevations: Low—47 feet on Peters Canyon Regional Trail & Bikeway adjacent to Harvard Community Park; high—298 feet at Irvine Boulevard and Sand Canyon Avenue
Traffic and hazards: Daily traffic volumes were 23,000 on Portola Parkway east of Jamboree Road, 25,000 on Irvine Boulevard between Jeffrey Road and Sand Canyon Avenue, 37,000 on Sand Canyon Avenue south of Trabuco Road, and 9,000 on Harvard Avenue between Walnut Trail and Como Channel Trail. Along Venta Spur Trail, there are two street crossings that require a detour.
Map: *The Thomas Guide by Rand McNally—Street Guide: Los Angeles and Orange Counties* (any recent year), page 860

Getting there by car: From central Anaheim, head south on I-5. Exit at Jamboree Road, on the Tustin/Irvine border, and turn right. Turn left on Walnut Avenue and then right on Harvard Avenue. Look for Harvard Community Park on the right.
Getting there by public transit: Metrolink trains serve Tustin Station, 1.2 miles from Harvard Community Park. There are three lines, with forty-two trains in each direction per day on weekdays and twenty-three trains in each direction per day on weekends. From the station, head southeast on Edinger Avenue. Left at Harvard Avenue and then left onto Como Channel Trail (paved path). The path bends 90° right, becoming Peters Canyon Regional Trail & Bikeway. Harvard Community Park is on the right, just up the path.
Starting point coordinates: 33.707272°N / 117.801642°W

The Ride

Upper Irvine–Northwood Nexus is a tour of northern Irvine, using bike paths and roads in that neck of the city. The 14.8-mile road ride layout is a clockwise loop. There are 383 feet of climbing along the way, but the climbing is gradual, with no steep gradients. The ride uses several of Irvine's paved bikeways, including Peters Canyon Regional Trail & Bikeway, West Irvine Trail, Peters Canyon Trail East Branch, Venta Spur Trail, Walnut Trail, and Como Channel

MASTER PLANNING A CITY

The city of Irvine has experienced pronounced growth since 1970—all part of the Master Plan. The city had a population of just 10,080 in 1970; folks who were around at that time would barely recognize the transformation. The population grew by an astonishing 20% per year during the 1970s, to 62,130 in 1980. The growth rate has slowed, but the number of persons being added every ten years has increased. Where will it end? The buildout projection of 250,000 has already been exceeded, and new construction continues. Irvine could become Orange County's largest city by, say, 2030. Part of the reason for the added growth is the decommissioning of Marine Corps Air Station El Toro in 1999. The availability of that land, possibility not foreseen when Irvine's plans were drawn up, has opened up new possibilities for construction. Another chunk of land, formerly occupied by Lion Country Safari—which was a drive-through animal preserve—has also been transformed with new construction. Irvine is now divided into more than forty-five villages, each with its own architecture, layout, parks, paths, and centers. Each village is a desirable residential location, and there are essentially no ghettos. There are no old buildings, so the entire city seems fresh and vibrant. And bicycling through Irvine along its many pathways is a pleasant experience.

Trail. Irvine's population was estimated to be 287,401 in 2019, exceeding the original buildout projection of 250,000 (please see sidebar). The start and finish are at Harvard Community Park in Walnut (one of Irvine's forty-five villages). As for those villages, the houses in Walnut have a Prairie design. From there, the ride passes through Lower Peters Canyon, Northwood (Bungalow and Craftsman-style houses), along the edge of Woodbury (French, Spanish, and Tuscan architecture), and Oak Creek Village (no prevailing style). West Irvine Trail, which the ride uses, parallels Jamboree Road for a stretch. The road is so named because the 1953 Boy Scouts Jamboree was held to the south of here in Newport Beach; the event was attended by over 30,000.

Miles and Directions

0.0 Start from west side of Harvard Community Park; head west on path to leave park.

0.1 Right on Peters Canyon Regional Trail & Bikeway (paved path); lowest elevation of ride (47 feet).

0.4 Pass under Walnut Avenue, Harvard Avenue (mile 0.55), I-5 (mile 1.0), El Camino Real (1.25), and Bryan Avenue (mile 1.5).

1.55 Turn sharply right, onto connector path.

1.6 End of connector path; right onto Bryan Avenue—cross over CA 261.

1.7 Right on West Irvine Trail (paved path).

2.15 Pass under Irvine Boulevard.

2.5 West Irvine Trail curves around cul-de-sac.

2.8 West Irvine Trail bends 90° right; now adjacent to Jamboree Road.

3.0 Traffic signal at Robinson Drive and at Trevino Drive (mile 3.3)—keep straight.

3.4 Trail approaches Valencia Park; stay left to remain on West Irvine Trail.

3.45 Pass under Jamboree Road.

3.7 Traffic signal at Champion Way—keep straight.

4.0 Leave West Irvine Trail at intersection between Portola Parkway and Jamboree Road (signalized); turn right (enter road) to head east-southeast on Portola.

4.3 Traffic signal at southbound CA 261 ramp and at northbound ramp (mile 4.4)—keep straight on Portola.

4.45 Right on Peters Canyon Trail East Branch (paved path).

5.4 T junction at Hicks Canyon Trail; turn right to continue on Peters Canyon Trail East Branch.

5.65 Pass under Irvine Boulevard.

5.9 Left onto Venta Spur Trail (paved path).

6.15 Cross Amargosa (paved residential road).

6.3 End of path at Rosenblum—keep straight onto Florence (paved residential road).

6.4 Traffic signal at Culver Drive—keep straight.

6.5 Venta Spur Trail resumes (keep straight).

6.8 Path arrives at Westwood (residential road)—no crossing here, so right on Westwood, cross at Mayflower, and then return on opposite side of Westwood to Venta Spur.

7.3 Path arrives at Yale (residential road)—no crossing here, so right on Yale, cross at Monticello, and then return on opposite side of Yale to Venta Spur.

7.7 Cross Eastwood (residential road)—keep straight.

8.2 End of Venta Spur Trail at Jeffrey Road; left onto Jeffrey's walkway.

8.45 Leave walkway at intersection of Jeffrey Road and Irvine Boulevard (signalized); turn right (enter road) to head east-southeast on Irvine.

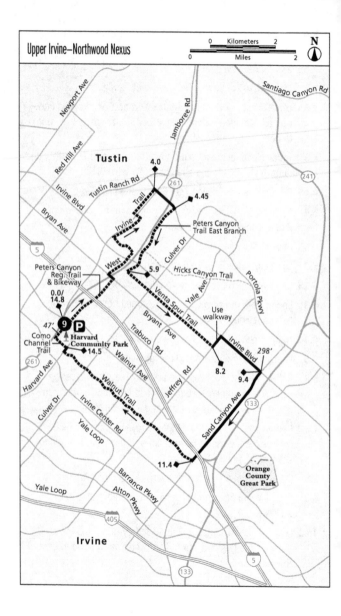

Kilometers

Miles

N

Newport Ave

Santiago Canyon Rd

Red Hill Ave

Tustin

4.0

Tustin Ranch Rd

261

241

Irvine Blvd

4.45

Trail

Bryan Ave

Irvine

Peters Canyon
Trail East Branch

5

West

Culver Dr

5.9

Hicks Canyon Trail

Peters Canyon
Reg. Trail
& Bikeway

Venta Spur Trail

Yale Ave

Portola Pkwy

0.0/
14.8

47'

9

P

Bryant Ave

Use
walkway

Como
Channel
Trail

Harvard
Community Park

Trabuco Rd

Irvine Blvd

298'

261

14.5

Walnut Ave

Jeffrey Rd

8.2

9.4

Harvard Ave

Walnut Trail

133

Culver Dr

Irvine Center Rd

Sand Canyon Ave

Yale Loop

11.4

Barranca Pkwy

Orange
County
Great Park

Yale Loop

Alton Pkwy

405

Irvine

133

5

8.95 Traffic signal at Groveland and at Virtuoso (mile 9.25)—keep straight.

9.4 Traffic signal at Sand Canyon Avenue—turn right; highest elevation of the ride (298 feet).

9.6 Traffic signal at Strata and at Towngate (mile 9.85), Trabuco Road (mile 10.35), Roosevelt (mile 10.6), Nightmist (10.85), I-5 freeway ramps (miles 11.1 and 11.15), and Burt Road (mile 11.3)—keep straight on Sand Canyon at each intersection.

11.35 Pass under Metrolink (railroad tracks).

11.4 Leave Sand Canyon Avenue; right on Walnut Trail (paved path).

12.35 Pass over Jeffrey Road.

13.1 Stay right at fork; pass under Yale Avenue and over Culver Drive (mile 13.95).

14.45 End of Walnut Trail at Harvard Avenue; right on Harvard—cross railroad tracks.

14.5 Left on Como Channel Trail (paved path).

14.75 Path curves 90° right, becoming Peters Canyon Regional Trail & Bikeway.

14.8 End of ride, adjacent to Harvard Community Park.

BIKE SHOPS

Jax Bicycle Center, 14210 Culver Dr., Heritage Plaza, Irvine, (949) 733–1212, www.jaxbicycles.com

Rock N Road Cyclery Irvine, 6282 Irvine Blvd., Woodbury Town Center, Irvine, (949) 733–2453, www.rock nroadcyclery.net

Trail's End Cycling Center, 17145 Von Karman Ave., Suite 108, Irvine, (949) 863–1982, http://trailsendcc.com

Southern Orange County is located to the south of Costa Mesa, Santa Ana, and Tustin. The subregion includes the cities of Aliso Viejo, Dana Point, Irvine, the four Lagunas (Beach, Hills, Niguel, and Woods), Lake Forest, Mission Viejo, Newport Beach, Rancho Santa Margarita, San Clemente, and San Juan Capistrano and the unincorporated communities of Coto de Caza, Emerald Bay, Ladera Ranch, Las Flores, and Rancho Mission Viejo. As of 2019 the largest city in southern Orange was Irvine at 287,401, followed by Mission Viejo at 94,381, and the region's total population was at just over one million, reflecting 30% of the county (and 40% of the area).

In 2019 the population density of southern Orange County, at about 3,300 per square mile, was substantially lower than northern Orange County's density of 6,900. Eleven of the book's rides are in southern Orange County. Southern Orange County's biggest attractions are its coastline, planned communities, Mission San Juan Capistrano, Irvine Spectrum (shopping and entertainment), Dana Point Harbor, Balboa Island, regional and state parks, park trails, and paths and trails linking communities and parks. Some of these are visited by the rides in this section. The diversity in southern Orange County is not nearly as great as that in northern Orange, perhaps because of or contributing to the population's generally conservative political bent. But there is an intriguing mix of cultures that ranges from the "content" (wealthy, exclusive, posh) to bohemian (heliophilic, artful, beach-bumming). You are bound to get a dose of both when you are out and about on your bicycle. Two road and four mountain bike rides are described in detail.

10 Arroyo Trabuco Sur-cuit

Start: Cox Sports Park, 27623 Crown Valley Parkway, Ladera Ranch

Length: 5.75 miles (pinched clockwise loop)

Riding time: 30 to 75 minutes (my time: 55:50 on foot)

Terrain and surface: 83% dirt trails, 12% paved roads, and 5% concrete paths

Elevations: Low—328 feet on Arroyo Trabuco Trail under Crown Valley Parkway overpass; high—571 feet on Arroyo Trabuco Trail adjacent to Santa Margarita Water District facilities

Traffic and hazards: The heaviest traffic volumes are on O'Neill Drive, which is a collector.

Map: *The Thomas Guide by Rand McNally—Street Guide: Los Angeles and Orange Counties* (any recent year), page 922

Getting there by car: From central Anaheim, head south on I-5. Exit at Crown Valley Parkway, in Mission Viejo, and turn left. Look for Cox Sports Park on the left, prior to arriving at O'Neill Drive.

Getting there by public transit: No transit service available

Starting point coordinates: 33.565714°N / 117.647756°W

The Ride

Arroyo Trabuco Sur-cuit is a 5.75-mile mountain bike ride in the young community of Ladera Ranch, in southern Orange County. The ride cruises along a southern segment of Trabuco Canyon, climbs out of it, descends back into it, and then climbs out of it a second time, to return to the start. The "Sur" in the ride title refers to its southerly location along the Arroyo Trabuco. The elevation differential is just 243 feet, but the two canyon ascents produce a total climb of 371 feet. The first climb (unnamed trail) is short (0.15 miles), at an average grade of 12.2%; the second descent,

LADERA RANCH

Growth in southern Orange County has continued at a staggering pace. Most of the growth has involved master planning. The plans have led to the construction of entire communities nestled in the southern Orange County foothills, generally with middle- to upper middle–class dwellings. All of the communities have taken advantage of the scenery and topography to establish parks, open space preserves, and trail systems—to protect native habitats and to facilitate public enjoyment and recreation. Coto de Caza, Ladera Ranch, Las Flores, Rancho Santa Margarita, and Rancho Mission Viejo are all now established settlements, each with thousands of residents. The two newest are Ladera Ranch and Rancho Mission Viejo. Ladera Ranch had an estimated population of 28,800 in 2017, up 25% since 2010. Construction began in 1999 on a 4,000-acre planned community, transforming what was once a large, working cattle ranch into livable space. The "ranch" now features nine villages, each with its own architectural theme, with all of the components of a complete and vibrant community.

on Waterworks Trail, is not steep but has a few curves, dips, and sun-to-shade segments. The ride starts and ends in Cox Sports Park. My measurements start from the far northern end of the parking lot. The route uses Ladera Ranch, Arroyo Trabuco, and Waterworks Trails, and an unnamed trail and connector. Arroyo Trabuco is a popular trail adjacent to a usually dry wash that extends for several miles to the north and south of this route.

Miles and Directions

0.0 Start the ride from the north end of the parking lot at Cox Sports Park in Ladera Ranch. Head south on Ladera Ranch Trail, which overlooks Trabuco Canyon.

0.15 Ladera Ranch Trail curves to the right, becoming a concrete path—begin descent (7.4% grade).

0.25 Trail curves to the left to pass under Crown Valley Parkway, followed by another curve to the left.

0.3 Concrete path climbs (12.4% grade).

0.4 Fence with narrow opening; pass through the opening, then turn right to cross the V drainage channel—head down the trail on the opposite side of the channel.

0.5 End of descent; turn right onto Arroyo Trabuco Trail (pass under Crown Valley Parkway; lowest elevation of the ride: 328 feet).

1.1 Curve right and then left to remain on Arroyo Trabuco Trail.

1.75 Keep straight at Waterworks Trail junction.

1.95 Turn right on unnamed trail; begin gradual climb.

2.05 Bear right at fork; trail enters a series of switchbacks (12.2% grade).

2.2 Grade of climb eases.

2.3 Stay left at fork.

2.45 Trail junction (multiple trails)—highest elevation of the ride: 571 feet; turn right onto trail that parallels solar panels.

2.6 Trail curves to the left—solar panels and Santa Margarita Water District facilities to the left.

2.7 Bear right onto unnamed connector trail; then stay right onto Waterworks Trail—begin descent.

3.35 End of Waterworks Trail—watch for rocks; turn left on Arroyo Trabuco Trail.

4.0 Turn left on concrete path—begin climb (9.0% grade).

4.15 Turn left on Ladera Ranch Trail.

4.35 Go left or right at the fork.

4.65 Leave Ladera Ranch Trail; turn right onto the connector, and continue onto Thalia Street (paved road).

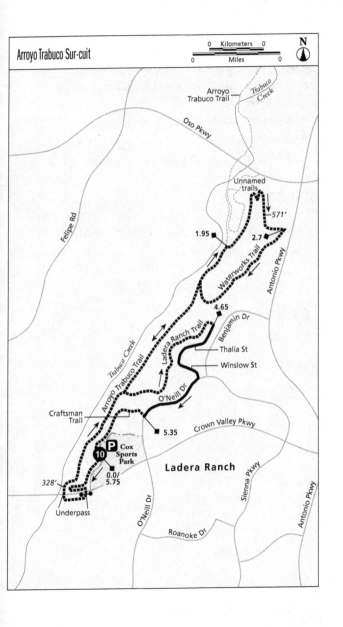

Arroyo Trabuco Sur-cuit

Kilometers

Miles

N

Arroyo
Trabuco Trail

Trabuco Creek

Oso Pkwy

Felipe Rd

Unnamed
trails

571'

1.95 ■

2.7 ■

Waterworks Trail

Antonio Pkwy

4.65 ■

Benjamin Dr

Ladera Ranch Trail

Thalia St

Winslow St

Trabuco Creek

Arroyo Trabuco Trail

O'Neill Dr

Craftsman
Trail

Crown Valley Pkwy

5.35 ■

P Cox
Sports
Park

10

Ladera Ranch

328'

0.0/
5.75 ■

Underpass

O'Neill Dr

Sienna Pkwy

Antonio Pkwy

Roanoke Dr

4.85 End of Thalia; continue across separator and onto Winslow Street.

5.05 After curving to the left, Winslow ends; continue across separator and onto O'Neill Drive—turn right on O'Neill (ride on shoulder).

5.35 Turn right at gate—continue on Craftsman Trail.

5.55 End of Craftsman; turn left on Ladera Ranch Trail.

5.75 End of ride, adjacent to Cox Sports Park parking lot.

BIKE SHOP

Bicisport Bicycles/Celo Europa Bicycles, 28940 Golden Lantern St., Suite A, Laguna Hills, (949) 643–1620, http://celoeuropa.net

11 Corona to Crystal Shoreline Ride

Start: Bayside Drive Park, Bayside Drive and Jasmine Avenue, Corona del Mar

Length: 7.1 miles (lollipop with "skinny" clockwise loop)

Riding time: 25 to 70 minutes (my time: 30:53)

Terrain and surface: 67% paved roads and 33% paved path

Elevations: Low—49 feet on Crystal Cove Trail, just north of Crystal Cove Shake Shack; high—128 feet on CA 1 at Pelican Point Drive

Traffic and hazards: The daily traffic volume on CA 1 in Corona del Mar was 34,000.

Map: The Thomas Guide by Rand McNally—Street Guide: Los Angeles and Orange Counties (any recent year), page 919

Getting there by car: From central Anaheim, head south on I-5.

Exit at CA 55 (freeway) and head south. Keep straight into Newport Beach via Newport Boulevard. Exit Newport to CA 1 (Pacific Coast Highway) and head south. In Corona del Mar, turn right on Marguerite Avenue, followed by a right on Bayside Drive. Bayside Drive Park is at right (park on street).

Getting there by public transit: OCTA bus route 1 runs along CA 1 between Long Beach and San Clemente, passing through Corona del Mar. Exit bus on CA 1 and head south on Iris Avenue, Jasmine Avenue, or Larkspur Avenue to Bayside Park. Service is provided every 35 minutes on weekdays and every hour on weekends and holidays.

Starting point coordinates: 33.596903°N / 117.872856°W

The Ride

Between Newport Beach and Laguna Beach are some extremely picturesque stretches of Southern California coastline. Corona to Crystal Shoreline Ride uses CA 1 and the Crystal Cove Trail (paved path) between Corona del Mar and Crystal Cove State Park. It is a 7.1-mile road ride, with

DUKE KAHANAMOKU

He was a native Hawaiian, but legendary surfer and swimmer Duke Kahanamoku (1890–1968) had a connection to Corona del Mar. Born in Honolulu, Duke grew up in Waikiki; his family was related to the Kamehamehas and they were considered to be low-ranking nobles. In 1912, Duke chopped nearly 8% off the world 100-yard freestyle swimming record, but his record was denied by the Amateur Athletic Union, in disbelief over the timing method and conditions. Duke nonetheless qualified for the US Olympic swimming team in 1912 and would win the gold medal in the 100-meter freestyle. His Olympic swimming career extended to 1924, with five cumulative medals. Duke nearly made the 1932 US Olympic water polo team, at age forty-two, qualifying as an alternate. Duke's "other" sport was surfing. He gave swimming exhibitions between Olympics and would throw in surfing demonstrations. His shows took him to Southern California and Australia. In 1925, while in Corona del Mar, a fishing vessel capsized in the harbor. Duke used his surfboard to rescue eight sailors. It was the first use of a surfboard in a rescue operation and led to their regular use by US lifeguards. Later in life, Duke served as the sheriff of Honolulu, from 1932 to 1961 (thirteen straight terms). There are statues of Duke in Hawaii and Australia; there is no statue of him in Corona del Mar, but maybe there should be!

a minor elevation change (79 feet). The ride starts in Corona del Mar at Bayside Drive Park. Corona del Mar is a community within the city of Newport Beach, with a population of about 12,500. Corona del Mar State Beach is just a few blocks from Bayside Park. After passing through Corona del Mar's busy retail district and a short stretch of residential development, CA 1 borders Crystal Cove State Park. There are open views of the ocean along here. After passing a number of entrances to the park, the route finally enters the park opposite Reef Point Drive. After a jaunt through the parking lot, the ride returns to Corona del Mar on Crystal Cove Trail, which is a paved bike path.

Miles and Directions

0.0 Start at Bayside Drive Park in Corona del Mar. From Bayside Drive and Jasmine Avenue, head southeast on Bayside.

0.1 Traffic signal at Marguerite Avenue—turn left.

0.15 Traffic signal at CA 1 (Pacific Coast Highway)—turn right; enter retail district.

0.45 Leave retail district; ride adjacent to residential neighborhoods.

1.25 Leave residential areas (right side of the road); Crystal Cove State Park at right—highest elevation of ride: 128 feet.

2.5 Crystal Cove Shake Shack at right—busy spot; queue of motor vehicles may extend onto CA 1. Begin short climb (3.3% grade).

3.25 Traffic signal at Reef Point Drive; turn right to enter Crystal Cove State Park.

3.35 Left at end of access road—ride to end of parking lot.

3.5 Right onto Crystal Cove Trail (paved path).

4.0 Stay right at fork.

4.4 Break in trail at Crystal Cove Shake Shack; leave walkway and ride in access road (watch for motor vehicles).

4.45 Return to path, beyond Shake Shack.

4.5 Lowest elevation of ride (49 feet).

4.75 Curve left to cross road.

5.0 Trail passes parking lot on right and state park facilities (including restrooms) on left—similarly at miles 5.25 and 5.45.

5.75 Stay right at fork in path.

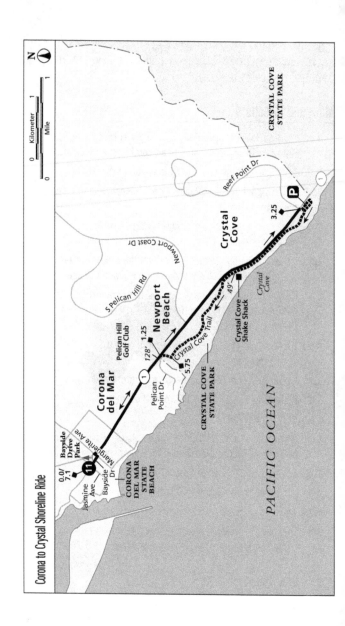

Corona to Crystal Shoreline Ride

5.85 End of Crystal Cove Trail at Pelican Point Drive and CA 1 (traffic signal)—turn left.

6.65 Return to Corona del Mar's retail district.

6.95 Traffic signal at Marguerite Avenue—turn left.

7.0 Traffic signal at Bayside Drive—turn right.

7.1 End ride at Jasmine Avenue, adjacent to Bayside Drive Park.

BIKE SHOP

Bikes 'N' Boards (bike rentals), 329 Marine Ave., Newport Beach, (714) 600–9941

12 Meandering Ladera Ridge

Start: Oak Tree Park, 25571 Meandering Trail, Las Flores
Length: 4.05 miles (clockwise loop with mid-route out-and-back)
Riding time: 30 to 75 minutes (my time: 60:44 on foot)
Terrain and surface: 60% dirt trails, 24% paved roads, and 16% concrete paths
Elevations: Low—589 feet at Oso Parkway and church access road; high—896 feet at junction of Ladera Ridge and Las Flores Ridge Trails
Traffic and hazards: Daily traffic volumes were 40,000 on Antonio Parkway near Las Flores Ridge Trail and 27,000 on Oso Parkway east of Antonio Parkway. There are loose rocks on Ladera Ridge Trail.
Map: *The Thomas Guide by Rand McNally—Street Guide: Los Angeles and Orange Counties* (any recent year), page 922
Getting there by car: From central Anaheim, head south on I-5. Exit at Oso Parkway, in Mission Viejo, and turn left. Left on Meandering Trail (paved road). Just past the crest, look for Oak Tree Park on the left.
Getting there by public transit: No transit service available
Starting point coordinates: 33.590958°N / 117.623608°W

The Ride

Meandering Ladera Ridge is a short (4.05-mile) but worthy mountain bike ride, 60% of which is on trails in Las Flores, in southern Orange County. The ride travels along Ladera Ridge. Ridge trails can be among the most challenging of trails, with rollercoaster profiles, but Ladera Ridge Trail is relatively tame. This ride reaches the highest elevation of any in this book (896 feet), and the total amount of climbing is 322 feet. The ride starts at Oak Tree Park in Las Flores. Las Flores is an unincorporated community, with a population of

CAÑADA CHIQUITA

While riding along Ladera Ridge—keeping your eyes on the trail— you may glance into the canyon to the east and wonder: "What's going on down there?" That collection of buildings in Cañada Chiquita is Tesoro High School, established in 2001. Although it seems remote, the school has an overcrowding problem, with over 2,500 students. The school thrives, though, with a high academic rating and a top-notch vocal program. Tesoro's Madrigals premiered a composition by Luke Mayernik—wonderfully entitled "Un Tesoro Perfecto"—at Carnegie Hall in 2013. The choir has toured Europe, and director Keith Hancock won a Grammy Educator of the Year Award In 2017. The school is just west of Los Patrones Parkway, which was originally planned as an extension of the CA 241 freeway southward to I-5, in Camp Pendleton. The base denied permission to build, however. Routing near San Onofre Beach State Park and the Donna O'Neill Land Conservancy generated further resistance. The parkway, which was under construction as of this writing, is a shorter alternative, with a parallel multipurpose pathway, wildlife crossings and fencing, and some new plantings. It may be upgraded and lengthened in the future, though, as volumes on I-5 continue to increase. Farther to the east of Cañada Chiquita are Thomas F. Riley Wilderness Park, which is toured in *Best Bike Rides Orange County*'s "Riley Five Miley" and Coto de Caza, where the 1984 Olympic Games's modern pentathlon events were held.

just under 6,000 as of 2010. The community is surrounded by Mission Viejo to the west, Rancho Santa Margarita to the north, Coto de Caza to the east, and Ladera Ranch to the south. When Rancho Santa Margarita incorporated as a city in 2000, Las Flores remained separate. Oak Tree Park is home to Las Flores Bike Jumps at Oak Tree Park, on the north side of the park. Catch some air after the ride! The ascent to Ladera Ridge Trail is an average 12.6% grade. It is a short climb—watch out for loose rocks. Also, the trail is rutted; a rut is a depression with short, steep walls on either side. The trail is wide enough for riding, though. The descent on Las Flores Ridge Trail is spectacular. Keep control of your bike and enjoy the ride. Always keep the tail of the bike stable and grounded; this usually requires sitting back on the saddle.

Miles and Directions

0.0   Start at Oak Tree Park in Las Flores; exit and turn right onto Meandering Trail (paved road).

0.3   Traffic signal at Oso Parkway—turn left (begin climb: 4.2% grade).

0.55 Right onto Ladera Ridge Trail (unmarked)—begin climb (12.6% grade).

0.7   Grade of climb eases; rutted trail—watch out for loose rocks and eroded spots.

0.85 Keep straight at trail junction.

1.35 Keep straight at junction with Las Flores Ridge Trail—highest elevation of ride: 896 feet.

1.75 Preserve boundary; turn around here.

2.15 Left on Las Flores Ridge Trail—begin descent, gradual and then steep.

2.8   End of trail at Antonio Parkway—turn right.

2.95 Traffic signal at Deerpath—turn right.

3.0   End of Deerpath (cul-de-sac); left onto church access road.

3.2   End of access road—right on Oso Parkway (lowest elevation of ride: 589 feet).

3.3   Traffic signal at Morning Trail—keep straight.

3.45 Right onto concrete connector path.

3.55 End of connector; turn sharply left—cross bridge over Oso Parkway.

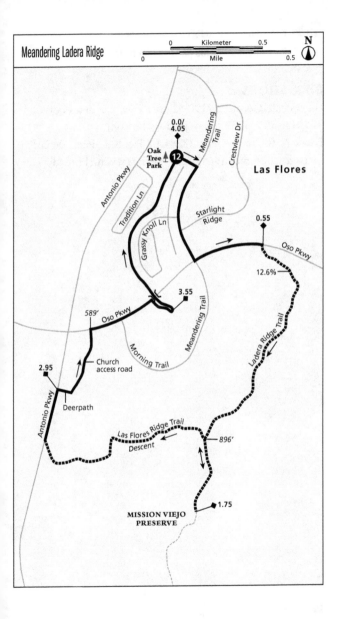

Meandering Ladera Ridge

Kilometer
0   0.5

Mile
0   0.5

N

Las Flores

Oak Tree Park

Antonio Pkwy

Tradition Ln

Grassy Knoll Ln

Meandering Trail

Crestview Dr

Starlight Ridge

0.0/ 4.05

12

0.55

12.6%

Oso Pkwy

589'

Church access road

Oso Pkwy

Morning Trail

Meandering Trail

Ladera Ridge Trail

2.95

Antonio Pkwy

Deerpath

Las Flores Ridge Trail
Descent

896'

1.75

MISSION VIEJO PRESERVE

3.55

3.85 Keep straight at merging path and at mile 3.9.

4.05 Path enters Oak Tree Park—end of ride.

BIKE SHOPS

Jax Bicycle Center, 27190 Alicia Pkwy., Laguna Niguel, (949) 364–5771, www.jaxbicycles.com

Rock N Road Cyclery, 27281 La Paz Rd., Plaza de la Paz, Laguna Niguel, (949) 360–8045, www.rocknroadcyclery .net

13 Oso Sweet SJC Trails Ride

Start: Northwest Open Space, 30291 Camino Capistrano, San Juan Capistrano

Length: 4.8 miles (clockwise loop)

Riding time: 30 to 75 minutes (my time: 62:59 on foot)

Terrain and surface: 70% dirt trails and 30% paved roads

Elevations: Low—113 feet at crossing of Oso Creek; high—286 feet along Oso Rancho Capistrano Trail

Traffic and hazards: The daily traffic volume on Camino Capistrano near Northwest Open Space was 6,000.

Map: The Thomas Guide by Rand McNally—Street Guide: Los Angeles and Orange Counties (any recent year), page 952

Getting there by car: From central Anaheim, head south on I-5. Exit at Avery Parkway, in Mission Viejo, and turn right. Left on Camino Capistrano and head south, entering San Juan Capistrano. Look for the entrance to Northwest Open Space on the right. Enter the park via the dirt road. Continue to staging area at end of road, adjacent to Joe D. Cortese Dog Park.

Getting there by public transit: OCTA bus route 91 travels between Laguna Hills and San Clemente, using Camino Capistrano in San Juan Capistrano, from which Northwest Open Space is easily accessed. Exit bus at the open space. Or make a bus-train connection at San Juan Capistrano Station, 2 miles to the south.

Starting point coordinates: 33.525758°N / 117.671039°W

The Ride

Oso Sweet SJC Trail Ride is a 4.8-mile mountain bike ride that heads toward the northwest corner of San Juan Capistrano, passing through the old, minimally developed 2C Ranch property. The start/finish is at Northwest Open Space (NOS). The old 2C Ranch was purchased in 2009 by

OSO CREEK

Although "Oso Sweet" has a nice ring to it, the more fitting phrase may be "Oso Sour," given the history of Oso Creek. Oso Creek is a tributary of Trabuco Creek, which is one of several tributaries of San Juan Creek. The mouth of San Juan is high in the Santa Ana Mountains. From there, the creek and its many tributaries eventually merge and flow into the Pacific Ocean. Decades of damming, reservoir development, and urbanization have stemmed the flow of the creeks and tributaries, though, such that the watershed is nowhere near its original, natural state. Oso lies on the western edge of the watershed. The Upper Oso Reservoir and Lake Mission Viejo were created from Oso Creek waters, transforming its flow into an ephemeral state (i.e., only after rainstorms). Oso merges with Trabuco Creek, which then merges with San Juan Creek, toward the southwestern edge of San Juan Capistrano. Although Oso is meant to be ephemeral, given the upstream damming, a constant flow is generated by urban runoff. Runoff typically contains particulates, sediments, liquid waste, and oils, so the creek waters are polluted. The "nuisance" waters are responsible for carving the 50-foot-deep(!) gorge that you pass on this ride. Although the gorge possesses some scenic beauty, it was originally only 6 feet deep and 6 feet wide—any further canyon carving is a threat to the orchards on the east side, and maybe even the bordering trail on the west side.

the city and promptly went neglected for a couple of years. Eventually, the newly formed San Juan Capistrano Open Space Foundation was able to make some improvements, leading to the opening of the NOS in 2012. In the title, SJC stands for San Juan Capistrano, and Oso is the name of a creek that the route crosses. The total amount of climbing on the ride is 303 feet, but the climbing is gradual. The opening Trabuco Creek Trail passes a large open space; it is slated for development of Putuidem Cultural Village, as a tribute to and replica of a community of the Acjachemen Nation. The Acjachemen lived in this area up to 12,000 years ago and were the original settlers. Oso Creek, which the ride crosses (mile 0.9), has a "nuisance" flow (please see sidebar). The creek environs can be thickly vegetated, and the trail narrows to single track. Starting at mile 1.95, along Oso Rancho Capistrano Trail, there is a 50-foot-deep gorge to the right (please see sidebar). It is a remarkable sight. Farther up the trail, the vegetation can be thick, with tall, overhanging reeds. After passing a peace garden, the ride enters a road that serves Saddleback Church Rancho Capistrano. After leaving the church grounds, it is a swift ride back on Camino Capistrano. At the entrance to NOS, Swanner House, on the right, is a local winery that is on the National Register of Historic Places.

Miles and Directions

0.0 Head south on Trabuco Creek Trail from staging area at Northwest Open Space.

0.45 Pass under railroad trestle and cross Trabuco Creek (concrete but rough).

0.5 Right to continue up short climb, remaining on Trabuco Creek Trail—Saddleback Valley Christian School at left.

0.8 Southern edge of school; bear right to descend into gulch—cross Oso Creek (wet crossing).

0.9 Stay right after crossing; single-track trail winds through thick, lush vegetation.

1.05 Turn left at top of short climb; head for clearing.

1.15 Stay right at clearing, in advance of tall reeds.

1.25 Turn sharply right—now on Oso Rancho Capistrano Trail; straight at next junction.

1.3 Trail climbs (8.9% grade); tall reeds should be at left.

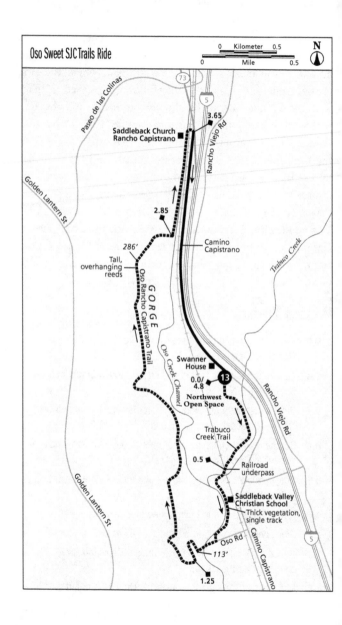

Oso Sweet SJC Trails Ride

Paseo de las Colinas

73

5

Rancho Viejo Rd

3.65

Saddleback Church Rancho Capistrano

Golden Lantern St

2.85

Camino Capistrano

286'

Tall, overhanging reeds

GORGE

Oso Rancho Capistrano Trail

Trabuco Creek

Oso Creek Channel

Swanner House

0.0/4.8

13

Northwest Open Space

Rancho Viejo Rd

Trabuco Creek Trail

0.5

Railroad underpass

Golden Lantern St

Saddleback Valley Christian School
Thick vegetation, single track

Oso Rd

113'

1.25

Camino Capistrano

5

0   Kilometer   0.5

0   Mile   0.5

1.65 Oso Rancho Capistrano Trail curves to the right; begin descent (5.1% grade).

1.95 Deep gorge (50 feet) at right; trail climbs (6.1% grade).

2.2 Stay left at fork—continue climb (7.8% grade)

2.3 Oso Rancho Capistrano Trail curves right—overgrown (tall reeds) when I rode this.

2.6 Highest elevation of ride (286 feet)—begin descent; emerge from heavy vegetation.

2.7 Trail curves sharply right—continue descent.

2.75 Pass by an old gate (open).

2.85 End of descent at trail junction; turn left to continue on Oso Rancho Capistrano Trail.

3.0 Peace garden at right—enter Saddleback Church Rancho Capistrano property.

3.1 Rudimentary parking area at left.

3.25 Leave parking area—right on church road (paved); road climbs, then curves right.

3.6 Pass through gate (open) and cross railroad bridge.

3.65 Right on Camino Capistrano.

4.45 Right to enter Northwest Open Space.

4.8 End ride at Northwest Open Space staging area.

BIKE SHOP

Buy My Bikes (South County Cyclery), 32302 Camino Capistrano, San Juan Capistrano, (949) 493–5611, http:// buymybikes.com

14 San Clemente Beach Boogie

Start: Max Berg Plaza Park, 1100 Calle Puente, San Clemente
Length: 5.85 miles (counter-clockwise loop)
Riding time: 25 to 60 minutes (my time: 49:50 on foot)
Terrain and surface: 61% paved roads and 39% dirt trail
Elevations: Low—12 feet on San Clemente Beach Trail adjacent to San Clemente Pier; high—168 feet on Ola Vista at Avenida Cordoba
Traffic and hazards: Daily traffic volumes were 2,460 on Avenida Calafia, 1,350 on Avenida Santa Barbara, 1,370 on Boca de la Playa, 2,570 on Ola Vista near Avenida Palizada, and 5,990 on Calle Puente north of Palizada. Be alert on the opening downhill on neighborhood roads. There are parking lots at both San Clemente Beach Trail termini—watch for maneuvering motor vehicles. On the trail, be cautious of other users, surfers crossing the trail carrying boards, sand encroachment, and erosion.
Map: *The Thomas Guide by Rand McNally—Street Guide: Los Angeles and Orange Counties* (any recent year), page 992
Getting there by car: From central Anaheim, head south on I-5. Exit at Avenida Pico in San Clemente; turn right. Left at El Camino Real. Right on Avenida Aragon, left at El Prado Avenue; Max Berg Plaza Park is at right—park on street.
Getting there by public transit: OCTA route 1 travels along CA 1 between Long Beach and El Camino Real in San Clemente. OCTA route 91 travels between Laguna Hills and San Clemente. Exit either bus on El Camino Real; head south on Avenida Aragon. Max Berg Plaza Park will be on the left. Route 1 runs every 35 minutes on weekdays and every hour on weekends and holidays. Route 91 runs every 30 minutes daily. San Clemente Station is located 1 mile from Max Berg Plaza Park. Metrolink operates three lines through the station, with forty-two trains in each direction on weekdays and twenty-three in each direction on weekends. Start the ride from

the station by heading through the parking lot and continuing directly onto San Clemente Beach Trail.

Starting point coordinates:
33.428306°N / 117.623103°W

The Ride

San Clemente Beach Boogie is a hybrid route, with 61% of the 5.85-mile route on paved roads and the other 39% on the dirt San Clemente Beach Trail. The path is immediately adjacent to San Clemente City Beach and San Clemente State Beach, providing excellent views of the ocean, the beaches, and San Clemente Pier. Expect to share the path with other users on all days—not just on weekends! As for the hybrid nature of the route, it is intended for a mountain or cyclocross bike, or even a road bike for skilled riders. Be aware that the beach trail occasionally has eroded spots, and that there can be sand encroachment from the beach. The ride starts and ends on road, at Max Berg Plaza Park in San Clemente. Max Lorenz Berg was a former San Clemente city clerk and the city's first Citizen of the Year. The park was named in his honor while he was still alive, long before he passed away at age ninety. The opening part of the bike ride is all downhill from the park to the beach. Exercise caution, as you could be carrying good speed amidst moving vehicles, parked vehicles, and motorists accessing driveways. The San Clemente Beach Trail trailhead is a busy hub, with folks walking to and from the beach, beach path users on foot and bicycle, surfers waxing or carrying their boards, train riders, and motorists making parking maneuvers. The dirt trail is 2.3 miles long and essentially flat. There are wooden bridges to cross at miles 1.4 and 3.1. The trail passes San Clemente Pier at mile 2.0. This is a *very* busy area, and cyclists are required

LA CASA PACIFICA

Beyond the end of San Clemente Beach Trail, fronting the ocean along the southern stretch of San Clemente State Beach, is La Casa Pacifica. The estate was known as the "Western White House" during President Richard M. Nixon's (1913-1994) tenure, from 1969 until 1974. President Nixon purchased the estate after taking office in 1969, when he was in search of a peaceful retreat. The estate's mansion was built in 1926 for Hamilton H. Cotton, one of the original financiers of the city of San Clemente. Cotton backed the Democratic Party and entertained President Franklin D. Roosevelt at the estate. During the time that President Nixon was in office, several luminaries visited La Casa Pacifica, including Soviet president Leonid Brezhnev, Japanese prime minister Eisaku Sato, Mexican president Gustavo Diaz Ordaz, and US secretary of state Henry Kissinger. After Nixon resigned in 1974—perhaps a Republican's purchase of property that was formerly owned by a Democrat was bad luck (kidding)—he and First Lady Patricia stayed at the estate, where he composed his memoirs. The 1977 David Frost-Richard Nixon interviews were originally scheduled to occur at La Casa Pacifica but had to be moved because of interference from US Coast Guard radio signals. Nixon sold the estate in 1980 to Allergan founder Gavin Herbert. As of this writing, Herbert had attempted to sell the property with no success. The estate is part of an exclusive, gated oceanside community and has never been open to the public.

to walk their bikes for about 300 feet, on the paved segment, until safely past the pier. Also, there are two at-grade crossings of the Metrolink track—at miles 1.8 and 2.45. Both crossings are controlled by a gate and audible warning. The beach trail ends at mile 3.3. It is all road from here, using the official San Clemente bike route that serves as an alternative to nearby El Camino Real, as a means of traveling north-south through the city. The route passes through predominantly residential neighborhoods, except for a brief crossing of Old Town. The route features a series of short uphills and downhills, along with a few curves. Be sure to follow the bike route signs. The ride crosses Avenida Del Mar at mile 5.3, which is the main drag of Old Town San Clemente.

Miles and Directions

0.0 Start at Max Berg Plaza Park in San Clemente—head north on Calle Puente.

0.1 Stop sign at Avenida Aragon—keep straight.

0.15 Stop sign at Avenida Pelayo—turn left.

0.3 Yield at Avenida Florencia—turn right.

0.45 Avenida Florencia curves left, becoming Calle Sacramento.

0.55 Stay right to merge with Calle Colina.

0.6 Calle Colina curves left.

0.65 Traffic circle at Boca de la Playa—bear right onto Boca de la Playa.

0.7 Left on Calle Deshecha—one-way street in your direction.

0.75 Stop sign at Avenida Pico—keep straight.

0.85 Stop sign at Avenida Estacion (end of Calle Deshecha)—turn left; enter parking area for train station and city beach.

1.0 End of Avenida Estacion—continue onto San Clemente Beach Trail (dirt).

1.4 Begin wooden bridge (0.2 miles long).

1.8 Trail curves sharply right to cross railroad track, then sharply left.

2.0 Trail enters San Clemente Pier area (paved segment)—cyclists must walk; lowest elevation of ride (12 feet).

2.05 Leave San Clemente Pier area—remount bicycle and resume dirt trail.

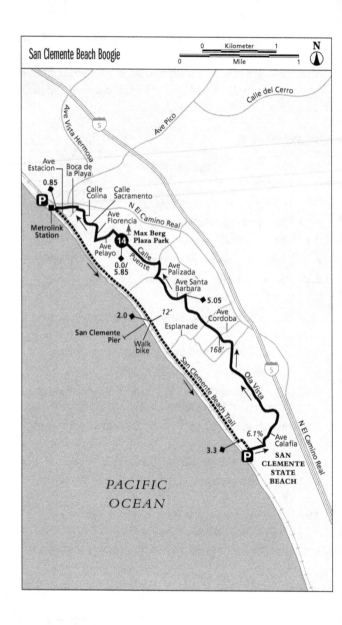

San Clemente Beach Boogie

0   Kilometer   1

0   Mile   1

N

Calle del Cerro

Ave Vista Hermosa

5

Ave Pico

Ave Estacion

Boca de la Playa

0.85

Calle Colina

Calle Sacramento

N El Camino Real

Metrolink Station

P

Ave Florencia

Ave Pelayo

14

Max Berg Plaza Park

0.0/ 5.85

Calle Puente

Ave Palizada

Ave Santa Barbara

5.05

2.0

12'

Ave Cordoba

Esplanade

San Clemente Pier

Walk bike

168'

San Clemente Beach Trail

Ola Vista

5

N El Camino Real

6.1%

Ave Calafia

3.3

P

SAN CLEMENTE STATE BEACH

PACIFIC OCEAN

2.45 Trail curves left to cross railroad track, followed by righthand bend.

3.1 Short wooden bridge.

3.3 End of San Clemente Beach Trail—bear left to enter parking area.

3.35 Bear right to leave parking area; climb Avenida Calafia (6.1% grade).

3.7 Left on Ola Vista—undulating road.

3.9 Stop sign at Avenida de la Riviera, at Avenida de los Lobos Marinos (mile 4.3), and at Avenida Valencia (mile 4.45)—keep straight on Ola Vista at these intersections.

4.65 Highest elevation of ride (168 feet) at Avenida Cordoba.

5.05 Stop sign at Avenida Santa Barbara—turn left.

5.15 Stop sign at Avenida Victoria and at Avenida Del Mar (mile 5.3)—keep straight on Santa Barbara.

5.4 Stop sign at Avenida Palizada—turn right.

5.55 Stop sign at Calle Puente—turn left.

5.85 End ride at Max Berg Plaza Park.

BIKE SHOPS

Bicycles San Clemente, 1900 N. El Camino Real, San Clemente, (949) 492–5737, www.urbanbicycleoutfitters.com

Jax Bicycle Center, 1421 N. El Camino Real, San Clemente, (949) 492–5911, www.jaxbicycles.com

15 Tour d'El Toro

Start: Orange County Great Park, 8000 Great Park Boulevard (parking lot 2, P2, adjacent to Hornet, between Phantom and Bosque), Irvine

Length: 11.6 miles (clockwise loop with short out-and-back segment)

Riding time: 35 to 90 minutes (my time: 44:19)

Terrain and surface: 100% paved roads

Elevations: Low—171 feet on Sand Canyon Road at Metrolink (railroad) underpass; high—451 feet on Irvine Boulevard at Magazine Road

Traffic and hazards: Daily traffic volumes were 19,000 on Irvine Boulevard adjacent to the old Marine Corps Air Station El Toro, 32,000 on Alton Parkway northeast of Technology Drive East, 17,000 on Technology Drive East, and 28,000 on Sand Canyon Road near I-5.

Map: *The Thomas Guide by Rand McNally—Street Guide: Los Angeles and Orange Counties* (any recent year), page 861

Getting there by car: From central Anaheim, head south on I-5. Exit at Sand Canyon Road, in Irvine, and turn left. Right on Marine Way. Left at Ridge Valley; right at Hornet. Park on the right, between Phantom and Bosque (P2; parking lot 2).

Getting there by public transit: Irvine Station, served by Metrolink trains, is located 4.2 miles from Orange County Great Park. The station is served by three lines, with forty-two trains in each direction on weekdays and twenty-three in each direction on weekends. Bicycle to Great Park from the station by heading west-northwest on Barranca Parkway and turning right on Technology Drive, right on Laguna Canyon Road, right on Sand Canyon Avenue, and right on Marine Way. Continue as above to Great Park.

Starting point coordinates: 33.511764°N / 117.633878°W

The Ride

Tour d'El Toro is an 11.6-mile urban road ride in the El Toro area of the city of Irvine. There are 318 feet of climbing along the way, but the elevation changes are gradual. Marine Corps Air Station (MCAS) El Toro was active from 1942 until 1999. The land was formerly owned by the Irvine Company; since decommissioning, the land has reverted to the city of Irvine. The former base covers 4,682 acres and was in the process of a long period of redevelopment as of this writing. Tour d'El Toro starts inside the former base, within redeveloped zones. The ride leaves those zones to travel along the base's perimeter and a bit beyond. The ride ends with a dash through

ORANGE COUNTY GREAT PARK

What to do with a 4,682-acre decommissioned military air base? Within a few years of the 1999 decommissioning of MCAS El Toro, plans had been made for a complete redevelopment. About 85% of the land is headed for residential and commercial uses and other infrastructure; 688 acres have been designated as Orange County Great Park. Plans were approved by county voters in 2002, for a proposed cost of $1.1 billion. Great Park's plans emphasize the arts and history, sports and recreation, some amusement attractions, and agriculture. The first attraction, Great Park Balloon, opened in 2007. The hot air balloon ascends to 500 feet and can carry up to thirty passengers. Other attractions include the Great Park Carousel, an arts complex, an aviation history exhibit, a farmers market, and facilities for baseball, basketball, ice skating, soccer, tennis, volleyball, and other "lawn" sports. There are some twenty-four soccer fields and twenty-five tennis courts! There is also a soccer stadium where a couple of pro teams play. Plenty of old maps, and Google Earth, were still showing a plan view of MCAS El Toro as of this writing.

Orange County Great Park (please see sidebar). Only a few years ago, most of the base was inaccessible, as it needed an environmental cleanup. After that period, with the base having limited access, there were bicycle races on segments of the old taxiways and runways. Those days passed quickly, as a major redevelopment effort moved forward. Today, the Orange County Great Park concept is partially complete, bringing with it enough of a road network to facilitate a bike route. On Irvine Boulevard, along the perimeter of MCAS El Toro, a newer development is Portola High School, on the right at mile 2.7. The school opened in the fall of 2016. As of this writing, because of its newness and the impacts of the coronavirus, the school was yet to have a set of students participate in a live graduation ceremony. Once back in Great Park, on the right, at mile 11.1—as of this writing—is the end of one of MCAS El Toro's old taxiways. During its heyday, the base's runways could accommodate any military jet; the longest runway was 10,000 feet. Be sure to check out Great Park's attractions.

Miles and Directions

- **0.0** Within Orange County Great Park, head north on Bosque from the traffic circle at Hornet and Bosque.

- **0.3** Traffic circle at Great Park Boulevard and at Cadence (mile 0.7)—continue northward on Bosque.

- **1.35** Traffic signal at Irvine Boulevard—turn right.

- **1.85** Traffic signal at Modjeska and at Pusan Way/Aquila Axis (mile 2.3), Chinon (mile 2.65), and Merit (mile 2.95)—keep straight.

- **3.3** Highest elevation of ride (451 feet) at Magazine Road.

- **3.65** Traffic signal at Alton Parkway—turn right.

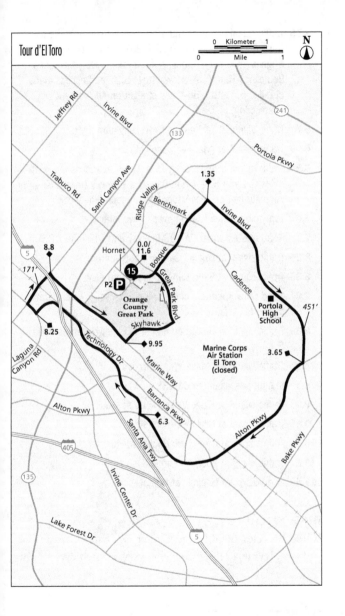

Tour d'El Toro

0 — Kilometer — 1
0 — Mile — 1

N

Jeffrey Rd
Irvine Blvd
241
Trabuco Rd
Sand Canyon Ave
133
Portola Pkwy
Ridge Valley
Benchmark
1.35
Irvine Blvd
5
171'
8.8
Hornet
0.0/ 11.6
Bosque
15
P2 P
Great Park Blvd
Cadence
Orange County Great Park
Portola High School
451'
8.25
Skyhawk
3.65
Laguna Canyon Rd
9.95
Technology Dr
Marine Way
Marine Corps Air Station El Toro (closed)
Barranca Pkwy
6.3
Santa Ana Fwy
Alton Pkwy
Alton Pkwy
Bake Pkwy
405
135
Irvine Center Dr
Lake Forest Dr
5

3.75 Traffic signal at Foster and at Fairbanks (mile 3.9), Bertea (mile 4.15), Toledo Way (mile 4.35), Morgan (mile 4.5), Hughes (mile 4.7), Jeronimo Road (mile 4.85), Muirlands Boulevard/Barranca Parkway (mile 5.2), and access roads at miles 5.4 and 5.55—keep straight on Alton at each intersection.

5.7 Traffic signal at Technology Drive East—turn right.

6.15 Traffic signal at Ada—keep straight.

6.3 Traffic signal at Technology Drive West, at access roads at miles 6.4 and 6.7, and at Barranca Parkway (mile 6.8)—keep straight on Technology East at each intersection.

7.6 Technology Drive East narrows to two lanes.

7.7 Road passes under CA 133 freeway and I-5 (mile 7.85).

8.25 Traffic signal at Laguna Canyon Road—turn right.

8.35 Traffic signal at Sand Canyon Road—turn right.

8.6 Sand Canyon passes under railroad tracks—lowest elevation of ride (171 feet).

8.65 Traffic signal at Burt Road and at I-5 freeway ramps (mile 8.7)—keep straight.

8.8 Traffic signal at Marine Way—turn right.

9.1 Marine passes under CA 133.

9.3 Traffic signal at Ridge Valley—keep straight.

9.95 Traffic signal at Skyhawk—turn left.

10.55 Traffic circle at Great Park Boulevard—turn left.

11.2 Traffic circle at Bosque—turn left.

11.6 End ride at traffic circle at Hornet.

BIKE SHOP

Irvine Bicycles, 6604 Irvine Center Dr., Sand Canyon Plaza, Irvine, (949) 453–9999, www.irvinebicycles.com

Honorable Mentions

The following are ten additional easy Orange County rides. Space limitations prohibited the inclusion of map and mileage logs for these. The text describes each route.

16 Angeles del Centro Santa Ana

What: 7.9-mile road ride. Start/finish: Angels Community Park, 914 West 3rd Street (also 300 North Flower Street), Santa Ana (33.746717°N / 117.877144°W). Elevation differential: 99 feet. Route: Clockwise loop from 3rd and Flower Streets via Flower Street to Warner Avenue, bike path to Pacific Electric Bike Trail, Raitt Street, 3rd Street to Angels Park. Note: No median opening at 3rd and Bristol.

17   Baker Ranch Promenade

What: 5.55-mile road ride. Start/finish: Passage Park, Mahogany and Wild Rose, Lake Forest (33.669700°N/ 117.674900°W). Elevation differential: 177 feet. Route: Lollipop plus a circle from park via Mahogany, Dimension Drive, traffic circle, bike-pedestrian path through Promenade Park, Laurel, Monarch Boulevard, Borrego Trail, Towne Center Drive South, Alton Parkway, Catalina, Laurel, path through Promenade Park, traffic circle, Monarch Boulevard, Alton Parkway, Catalina, traffic circle, Dimension Drive, Mahogany to Passage Park.

18 Balboa Peninsula Tour

What: 10.15-mile road ride. Start/finish: 38th Street Park, 38th and West Balboa Boulevard, Newport Beach (33.617906°N / 117.935206°W). Elevation differential: 7 feet. Route: Figure eight from the east side of the park via Park Lane, 38th Street, West Balboa Boulevard, McFadden Place, Newport–Balboa Bike Trail, E Street, East Balboa Boulevard, G Street, East Ocean Front, Channel Road, East Balboa Boulevard, Main Street, East Bay Avenue, West Bay Avenue, 15th Street, access road then path through Marina Park, West Bay Avenue (on other side of park), 19th Street, Newport-Balboa Bike Trail, through parking area, Ocean Front West (bike path), 36th Street, Seashore Drive, Orange Street, West Balboa Boulevard to 38th Street Park.

19 Capistrano's Crowl Prowl

What: 4.6-mile mountain bike ride. Start/finish: San Juan Capistrano Sports Park, 1 Via Positiva, San Juan Capistrano (33.489542°N / 117.676947°W). Elevation differential: 248 feet. Route: Clockwise loop via Via Positiva, Camino del Avion, Del Obispo Street, Paseo de la Paz, connector trail, Peppertree Trail, Trabuco Creek (West Bank) Trail, short connector near Del Obispo Street, Via Alipaz, Via Positiva to Sports Park.

20 Coastin' Costa Mesa

What: 13.25-mile road ride. Start/finish: West Newport Park, 5700 Seashore Drive, Newport Beach (33.624778°N / 117.946986°W). Elevation differential: 47 feet. Route: Lollipop plus a short loop via Seashore Drive, Orange Street, CA 1, Banning Channel Bikeway, bridge over channel, Santa Ana River Trail (SART), connector to MacArthur Boulevard, MacArthur Boulevard (across bridge), connector to SART on opposite side, SART, CA 1 (northwest), Brookhurst Street, Amarus Salt Marsh path, SART (pass under CA 1), CA 1 (use walkway, southeast), Orange Street, Seashore Drive to West Newport Park.

21 Cycle Serrano Creek

What: 6.3-mile mountain bike ride. Start/finish: Heritage Hill Historical Park, 25151 Serrano Road, Lake Forest (33.646639°N / 117.689278°W). Elevation differential: 371 feet. Route: Out-and-back from park via access road behind retail center, Trabuco Road (walkway—cross at Peachwood), Serrano Creek Trail to T junction at mile 3.1, climb hill to gate; turn around and return via the same route.

22 San Onofre Bluffs Blast

What: 7.3-mile mountain bike ride. Start/finish: San Onofre Trail 6 parking area, San Onofre State Beach (33.336447°N / 117.504353°W). Elevation differential: 163 feet. Route: Skinny loop with two out-and-back spurs—south on road from parking area, right at fence, right on trail; head northwest (wide trail with short, single-track segments). Leave trail at miles 1.5 and 3.25 to descend to beach and return. Near State Beach entrance (mile 4.55), return on roadway to start.

23 Santa Ana River Diversion

What: 8.5-mile mountain bike ride. Start/finish: Yorba Linda Regional Park (west entrance), 7600 East Palma Avenue, Yorba Linda (33.864681°N / 117.773647°W). Elevation differential: 59 feet. Route: Figure eight via connector to Santa Ana River Trail (SART, dirt; eastbound), 180° turn to SART (paved, westbound), connector near start to SART (dirt, westbound), bridge over river, SART (paved, westbound), Imperial Woods Trail (Imperial Wetlands Trail) to end, 180° turn to SART (paved, eastbound), bridge, SART (paved) to Yorba Linda Park.

24 **Seal Beach Wildlife to Weapons Loop**

What: 15.3-mile road ride. Start/finish: Sunset Harbour, 2901 Edinger Avenue, Sunset Beach (Huntington Beach) (33.727861°N / 118.077719°W). Elevation differential: 33 feet. Route: Clockwise loop with a short out-and-back via Park Circle Drive, Sunset Way, Edinger Avenue, Saybrook Lane, Heil Drive, Algonquin Street, Warner Avenue, CA 1, Seal Beach Boulevard, Westminster Boulevard, bike path adjacent Rancho Road, Bolsa Chica Road (walkway to McFadden Avenue, then bike lane), Edinger Avenue, Sunset Way, Park Circle Drive to Sunset Harbour.

25 Velo Capistrano

What: 9.4-mile road ride. Start/finish: Old Majors Field, 26898 Acjachema Street, San Juan Capistrano (33.505150°N / 117.660175°W). Elevation differential: 269 feet. Route: Clockwise loop via Acjachema Street, Camino Capistrano, Avery Parkway, Trabuco Creek bike path, Trabuco Creek Road, unnamed road opposite Rosenbaum, bike path parallel to Rancho Viejo Road (transfer to road at Mission Hills Road; return to path 0.6 miles later, or remain in road), Calle Arroyo, Paseo Tirador, San Juan Creek bike path, exit to Camino Capistrano, El Camino Real, Acjachema Street to Old Majors Field.

Want more? The following rides in *Best Bike Rides Orange County, California*, are classified as easy: Circle Newport Bay (road), Fairview-Talbert Nature Spin (mountain), Harriett Wieder Trails Express (mountain), and Riley Five Miley (mountain).

References

Books, Articles, and Reports

Berg, Tom. "How Irvine Became America's Best Planned City." *Irvine Standard*, September 26, 2018. www.irvine standard.com/2018/the-story-of-irvine. Retrieved December 2019.

California Department of Transportation. *2018 Traffic Volumes on the California State Highway System*. Division of Traffic Operations, California State Transportation Agency, State of California, Sacramento, 2019.

Chambers, Bruce. "This Way to Orange County's Redwood Forest." *Orange County Register*, March 11, 2013.

City of San Clemente, California. *City of San Clemente Average Daily Traffic*. Prepared by Transportation Studies, Inc., Tustin, CA, 2019. www.san-clemente.org/Home/ShowDocument?id=6578.

Davis, David. *Waterman: The Life and Times of Duke Kahanamoku*. Lincoln: University of Nebraska Press, 2015.

Delaney, Jeff. *Newport Beach: Then & Now*. Charleston, SC: Arcadia Publishing, 2011.

Greater Irvine Chamber. "Irvine Master Plan." https://www.greaterirvinechamber.com/irvine-master-plan. Retrieved December 2019.

Green, Dennis. "No One Wants to Buy Richard Nixon's 'Western White House.'" *Business Insider*, February 2, 2017. www.businessinsider.com/nixon-western-white -house-asks-63-million-2017-2. Retrieved on February 6, 2020.

"Max Lorenz Berg." *Orange County Register* obitu-
    ary, September 15, 2015. obits.ocregister.com/
    obituaries/orangecounty/obituary.aspx?n=max
    -lorenz-berg&pid=175835721&fhid=9225. Retrieved
    November 2019.

Meadows, Don. *Historic Place Names in Orange County*. Bal-
    boa Island, Newport Beach, CA: Paisano Press, 1966.

Mendoza, Raymond. "Fountain Valley, a Nice Place to Live."
    Orange County Register, July 10, 2014. www.ocregister
    .com/2014/07/10/fountain-valley-a-nice-place-to-live.
    Retrieved October 2019.

Molina, Alejandra. "Irvine Surpasses 250,000 Population
    Mark." *Orange County Register*, May 6, 2015.

Morris, Christina. "National Treasures: Historic Winters-
    burg." National Trust for Historic Preservation. https://
    savingplaces.org/places/historic-wintersburg#.WuuS_
    Jch2M8. Retrieved October 2019.

Nendel, James D. "Duke Kahanamoku: 20th Century
    Hawaiian Monarch." PhD diss., The Pennsylvania State
    University, 2006.

Noss, Reed F. ed. *The Redwood Forest: History, Ecology, and
    Conservation of the Coast Redwoods*. Washington, DC:
    Island Press, 2000.

Palmer, Mike. "The Yorba Linda Branch: Brea to Yorba
    Linda, CA." June 10, 2010. www.abandonedrails.com/
    Yorba_Linda_Branch. Retrieved October 2019.

Pierceall, Kimberly. "Irvine Great Park Plan Gets Plan-
    ners' OK." *Orange County Register*, July 18, 2014. www
    .ocregister.com/articles/plan-629203-park-irvine.html.
    Retrieved November 2019.

Pignataro, Anthony. "The Orange County Great Park Is
    Huge, Perfectly Manicured and Beautiful. So Where's

the Actual Park?" *OC Weekly*, August 16, 2018. www
.ocweekly.com/the-orange-county-great-park-is-huge
-perfectly-manicured-and-beautiful-so-wheres-the-actu
al-park. Retrieved on February 6, 2020.

San Juan Capistrano Open Space Foundation. "A Look
Back at 2011," Spring 2012 newsletter. www.sjcopen
spacefoundation.org/newsletters/newsletter_spring
_2012.html. Retrieved November 2019.

Schlom, Corey. *The Unseen OC: The Untold History, Stories,
and Legends of the Unseen Orange County*. Philadelphia,
PA: JPS Publishing, 2010.

Schrader, Esther. "Placentia Looking Up in Quest for Landmarks." *Los Angeles Times*, September 30, 1997. http://
articles.latimes.com/1997/sep/30/new/mn-37736.
Retrieved November 2019.

Schwartz, Bob. "Tour de Orange County: Santa Ana
River Trail Takes Bicyclists from the Canyons to the
Coast." *Los Angeles Times*, May 26, 1989. www.latimes
.com/archives/la-xpm-1989-05-26-li-889-story.html.
Retrieved November 2019.

Strawther, Larry. *Seal Beach: A Brief History*. Charleston, SC:
The History Press, 2014.

Urashima, Mary F. Adams. *Historic Wintersburg in Huntington
Beach*. Charleston, SC: The History Press, 2014.

Walser, Lauren. "Racing to Save Japanese-American History at Historic Wintersburg Village." National Trust
for Historic Preservation, February 19, 2014. https://
savingplaces.org/stories/race-save-japanese-american-
history-historic-wintersburg-village. Retrieved
October 2019.

Winslow, Jonathan. "Historic Wintersburg Makes National
List." *Orange County Register*, June 23, 2014. www

.ocregister.com/2014/06/24/historic-wintersburg-makes-national-list. Retrieved October 2019.

Yi, Daniel. "Irvine Wins Bid to Annex El Toro Site." *Los Angeles Times*, November 13, 2003. https://www.latimes.com/archives/la-xpm-2003-nov-13-me-eltoro13-story.html. Retrieved November 2019.

Websites

Individual Orange County city websites (information on city history, parks, streets, bicycle routes, and traffic volumes): Brea, Costa Mesa, Fountain Valley, Fullerton, Huntington Beach, Irvine, La Habra, Lake Forest, Newport Beach, Orange, Placentia, San Clemente, San Juan Capistrano, and Santa Ana.

National Register of Historic Places, www.nationalregisterofhistoricplaces.com.

Orange County Model Engineers, www.ocmetrains.org/welcome.html.

Orange County Parks, http://ocparks.com. Articles on Carbon Canyon, Heritage Hill Historical, Irvine, and Santiago Oaks Regional Parks.

Orange County Transportation Authority, Annual Traffic Flow Map, 2018, www.octa.net/pdf/2018-ADT.pdf.

Orange County Transportation Authority, Complete Bus Book, 2019, www.octa.net/ebusbook/CompleteBusBook.pdf.

Orange County Transportation Authority, Orange County Bikeways Map, www.octa.net/pdf/OCBikewaysMap.pdf.

Rails-to-Trails Conservancy, www.railstotrails.org.

Wikipedia articles (http://en.wikipedia.org) on Balboa Peninsula, Brea, Brea-Olinda Oil Field, California

State University Fullerton, cities in Orange County, Duke Kahanamoku, Fountain Valley, Fullerton, Fullerton College, La Habra, La Habra High School, Huntington Beach, Irvine, La Casa Pacifica, Ladera Ranch, Lake Forest, Las Flores, Lion Country Safari, largest California cities by population, Naval Weapons Station Seal Beach, Newport Beach, Orange, Orange County, Orange County Great Park, Orange Park Acres, Placentia, San Clemente, San Juan Capistrano, San Juan Creek, Santa Ana, Santa Ana River, Seal Beach, Sequoia sempervirens, Tustin, Valencia High School (Placentia), and Yorba Linda.

Ride Index

About the Author

Wayne D. Cottrell is an engineering, math, and science educator specializing in transportation, and a researcher, author, runner, cyclist, snowshoer, and orienteer. He is a member of the Transportation Research Board's Bicycle Transportation Committee and has been an active cyclist and member of USA Cycling for twenty-five years. His bicycle racing résumé includes a few road, cyclocross, and mountain bike wins and podium finishes. He won an award for his writing from the National Research Council in 1999. Wayne grew up in the Bay Area, in Oakland. He bicycled to college, then occasionally to work after graduating, and then for recreation and competition, becoming familiar with biking routes throughout California. Wayne is the author of FalconGuides for Utah, the Bay Area, Los Angeles, and Orange County; seventeen articles on transportation in refereed technical journals; thirty technical articles in conference proceedings; and a number of transportation research reports. He earned a PhD in transportation engineering from the University of Utah in 1997 and is a registered traffic engineer in California. Wayne is a licensed Category 3 and Masters cyclist with USA Cycling. He currently resides in Searles Valley, California.

CPSIA information can be obtained
at www.ICGtesting.com
Printed in the USA
LVHW052114241120
672597LV00014B/2003